KU-526-779

LawExpress
EU LAW

Develop your legal skills

9781408226100

9781447905141

9781408261538

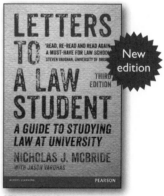

9781447922650

Written to help you develop the essential skills needed to succeed on your course and prepare for practice.

Available from all good bookshops or order online at:
www.pearsoned.co.uk/law

ALWAYS LEARNING

PEARSON

EU LAW

4th edition

Dr Ewan Kirk
Birmingham City University

Law Express

Class No.	341.2422 KIR
Site	RC 180953
Processed by	A&V
Approved by	EB

PEARSON

Harlow, England • London • New York • Boston • San Francisco • Toronto • Sydney • Auckland • Singapore • Hong Kong
Tokyo • Seoul • Taipei • New Delhi • Cape Town • São Paulo • Mexico City • Madrid • Amsterdam • Munich • Paris • Milan

Pearson Education Limited
Edinburgh Gate
Harlow CM20 2JE
United Kingdom
Tel: +44 (0)1279 623623
Web: www.pearson.com/uk

First published 2009 (print and electronic)
Second edition published 2011 (print and electronic)
Third edition published 2013 (print and electronic)
Fourth edition 2015 (print and electronic)

© Pearson Education Limited 2009, 2011, 2013, 2015 (print and electronic)

The right of Ewan Kirk to be identified as author of this work has been asserted by him in accordance with the Copyright, Designs and Patents Act 1988.

The print publication is protected by copyright. Prior to any prohibited reproduction, storage in a retrieval system, distribution or transmission in any form or by any means, electronic, mechanical, recording or otherwise, permission should be obtained from the publisher or, where applicable, a licence permitting restricted copying in the United Kingdom should be obtained from the Copyright Licensing Agency Ltd, Saffron House, 6–10 Kirby Street, London EC1N 8TS.

The ePublication is protected by copyright and must not be copied, reproduced, transferred, distributed, leased, licensed or publicly performed or used in any way except as specifically permitted in writing by the publishers, as allowed under the terms and conditions under which it was purchased, or as strictly permitted by applicable copyright law. Any unauthorised distribution or use of this text may be a direct infringement of the author's and the publishers' rights and those responsible may be liable in law accordingly.

Contains public sector information licensed under the Open Government Licence (OGL) v2.0. www.nationalarchives.gov.uk/doc/open-government-licence.

Pearson Education is not responsible for the content of third-party internet sites.

ISBN: 978-1-292-01289-6 (print)
      978-1-292-01341-1 (PDF)
      978-1-292-01811-9 (ePub)
      978-1-292-01307-7 (eText)

British Library Cataloguing-in-Publication Data
A catalogue record for the print edition is available from the British Library

Library of Congress Cataloging-in-Publication Data
Kirk, Ewan, author.
   EU law / Dr Ewan Kirk, Birmingham City University. -- 4th edition.
      pages cm. -- (Law express)
   Includes bibliographical references and index.
   ISBN 978-1-292-01289-6
   1. Law--European Union countries--Outlines, syllabi, etc.   I. Title.
   KJE947.K57 2014
   341.242'2--dc23
                              2014008984

10 9 8 7 6 5 4 3 2 1
18 17 16 15

Print edition typeset in 10/12pt Helvetica Neue LT Std by 35
Print edition printed and bound in Great Britain by Ashford Colour Press Ltd

NOTE THAT ANY PAGE CROSS REFERENCES REFER TO THE PRINT EDITION

Contents

Supporting resources

Visit the *Law Express* series companion website at **www.pearsoned.co.uk/lawexpress** to find valuable student learning material including:

- A **study plan** test to help you assess how well you know the subject before you begin your revision.
- Interactive **quizzes** to test your knowledge of the main points from each chapter.
- Sample **examination questions** and guidelines for answering them.
- Interactive **flashcards** to help you revise key terms, cases and statutes.
- Printable versions of the **topic maps** and **checklists** from the book.
- **'You be the marker'** allows you to see exam questions and answers from the perspective of the examiner and includes notes on how an answer might be marked.
- **Podcasts** provide point-by-point instruction on how to answer a typical exam question.

Also: The companion website provides the following features:

- Search tool to help locate specific items of content
- E-mail results and profile tools to send results of quizzes to instructors
- Online help and support to assist with website usage and troubleshooting

For more information please contact your local Pearson Education sales representative or visit **www.pearsoned.co.uk/lawexpress**

Acknowledgements

I'd like to thank all those who reviewed and offered feedback on chapters in this book, as well as Donna Goddard for her support and patience.

Finally, and most importantly, Penny.

Publisher's acknowledgements

Our thanks go to all reviewers who contributed to the development of this text, including students who participated in research and focus groups which helped to shape the series format.

Introduction

With the rapid development and expansion of the EU, it is becoming more important (if that is possible) for law students to get to grips with EU law. Rules and principles from the EU now affect an ever-expanding list of areas of law as powers are exercised and rules are made by the EU as a whole for the benefit of its Member States. It is also an area of law which is rapidly changing and has become very topical – the Lisbon Treaty is probably the most significant change to have occurred in the last few years, and has not been without controversy. Because of this, it is important to ensure that the sources you are using are as up-to-date as possible – older textbooks will have little or no reference to Lisbon and the changes this Treaty made.

The EU is also a very different system from the one you will have studied as part of your coursework on the English legal system. For this reason it appears daunting or 'scary' to many law students. However, this is not the case – EU law is, in some respects, more straightforward than the law in the UK, and a lot more linear. Students often make the mistake of attempting to draw parallels between the English legal system and the EU system. Although there are some parallels that can be safely drawn, you should not fall into the trap of thinking that the EU is just like the system in the UK – they are very different. As the UK was not a member of the EU when it was originally formed, many of the legal principles will be different as they are based upon the legal systems of some of the original six Member States.

EU law, however, overlaps and connects with other subjects in such a way that it has an effect on just about every area of law you will encounter on a law degree, and therefore it is important to get to grips with the basics of the topic not only for the examinations you will have in this subject, but to help you to gain a better understanding in those other areas. As the areas in which EU law-making grows, so will the influence of this area in other subjects. EU law and policy-making has grown significantly over the past few years, and so there is now a lot more law in the UK which has its foundation in the EU. What the study of EU law as a whole should give you is the familiarity and confidence to study the EU-based aspects of other subjects when you encounter them.

EU law can be broadly split into two general categories – first there are those aspects that concern the constitutional law of the EU, and secondly those that concern substantive elements of EU law (such as competition law, for example). You should bear in mind that no EU course will take you through all aspects of EU law, as there is such a wide range of topics covered, and much of the substantive law will appear in your other law subjects anyway.

This book aims to take you through the main areas studied by law students on LL.B degrees in the UK in the area of EU law, both concerning the way in which the EU legal system works, and substantive law subjects. EU law courses vary greatly between institutions, however, so there may be some difference between the content of this book and the syllabus of your course. However, common areas of EU law are covered here, and so you should use this book for what it is – a guide to the main areas in this subject required for you to do well. A word of warning – it is no substitute for your textbooks, your lecture notes and other materials: instead this book should help you to focus in your use of those other materials.

Finally, as mentioned above, you should be very careful in your use of out-of-date textbooks in EU law – the law changed rapidly and significantly in 2009. That is not to say you shouldn't use wider materials – just be aware that if something was published prior to the accession of the Lisbon Treaty in 2009, it needs to be read in conjunction with a more recent book in order to ensure you are not using out-of-date law. Your own textbook should certainly be one which has up-to-date law in it; otherwise you are going to get rather confused.

📖 REVISION NOTE

Things to bear in mind when revising EU law:

- EU law is becoming more important as more powers are given to the EU and EU law affects other areas of law.
- Don't think that the EU is just like the UK legal system – it is very different and has its own rules and traditions.
- There are legal system and substantive aspects of EU law – make sure you check the syllabus of your course to see where you should focus your study of EU law.
- Make sure that you make full use of your textbooks and lecture notes in order to understand the subject in depth – this book will not give you everything you need on its own.
- Make sure you practise essay/problem questions, and get feedback on how you are doing.

Before you begin, you can use the study plan available on the companion website to assess how well you know the material in this book and identify the areas where you may want to focus your revision.

Guided tour

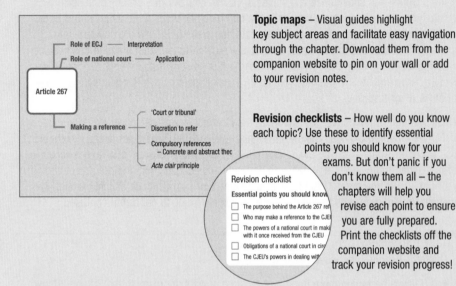

Topic maps – Visual guides highlight key subject areas and facilitate easy navigation through the chapter. Download them from the companion website to pin on your wall or add to your revision notes.

Revision checklists – How well do you know each topic? Use these to identify essential points you should know for your exams. But don't panic if you don't know them all – the chapters will help you revise each point to ensure you are fully prepared. Print the checklists off the companion website and track your revision progress!

Sample questions with answer guidelines – Practice makes perfect! Read the question at the start of each chapter and consider how you would answer it. Guidance on structuring strong answers is provided at the end of the chapter. Try out additional sample questions online.

Sample question

Could you answer this question? Below is a typical essay question that could arise on this topic. Guidelines on answering the question are included at the end of this chapter, whilst a sample problem question and guidance on tackling it can be found on the companion website.

Assessment advice – Not sure how best to tackle a problem or essay question? Wondering what you may be asked? Use the assessment advice to identify the ways in which a subject may be examined and how to apply your knowledge effectively.

ASSESSMENT ADVICE

When Article 267 is the sole area examined in a question, it will commonly be dealt with as an essay, although it may also form part of a question which touches on other areas as well.

Essay questions

Both essay and problem questions can focus upon the relationship between the national court and CJEU generally, or concentrate upon one aspect of the procedure. The development of the principles surrounding the issue of what a court of last instance constitutes, or discussion of the *CILFIT* principle (see Case 283/81 *CILFIT and Others* v *Ministro della Sanità* [1982] ECR 3415) which gives us criteria where a

Key definitions – Make sure you understand essential legal terms. Use the flashcards online to test your recall!

KEY DEFINITION: Court of last instance

A court of last instance is the last court in a particular court structure to which cases can go. Therefore, this means that once the case has been heard by this court, there is no route of appeal to another court. The Supreme Court, as the highest court in England and Wales, is the best example of a court in the UK court system that will *always* come under this definition.

Key cases and key statutes –
Identify and review the
important elements of the
essential cases and statutes
you will need to know for your
exams.

KEY STATUTE

Article 267 TFEU
The Court of Justice shall
■ the interpretation of th
■ the validity and interp
   the Union.
Where such a quest
court or tribunal

KEY CASE

Commissioners of Customs & Excise v Samex Aps [1983] 3 CMLR 194
Concerning: appropriateness of reference to CJEU; questions to raise

Facts

This case concerned the High Court's attempts to deal with European Regulations
concerning an import licence that one of the parties, an acrylic yarn importer, was
attempting to secure. In its deliberations, the court discussed the appropriateness of
a reference to the ECJ (now CJEU), and what questions would be in order.

Make your answer stand out – This
feature illustrates sources of further thinking
and debate where you can maximise your
marks. Use them to really impress your
examiners!

✓ Make your answer stand out

Because the *Arsenal* case was overruled by the Court of Appeal, the principle (above)
isn't given very much gravity – however, the principle is an important one, and goes
to the heart of the Article 267 procedure. The CJEU must not overstep its role in
this procedure to the detriment of the national court's sovereignty. It must stick to
interpretation, and not engage in applying the law to the facts. The importance of the
CJEU's contribution is in the interpretation, as it is recognised that in order to ensure

Exam tips – Feeling the pressure? These
boxes indicate how you can improve your
exam performance when it really counts.

EXAM TIP

Although it may seem to be an obvious definition when answering a problem question,
it is important to be able to establish definitively that a particular court or tribunal falls
within the definition under Article 267, especially as this differs from national ideas of
'court or tribunal'. Don't assume that the examiner will consider this issue obvious. It is
much better for you to discuss the issue to show that you have understood how it has
been applied by the CJEU.

Revision notes – Get guidance for effective
revision. These boxes highlight related
points and areas of overlap in the subject,
or areas where your course might adopt a
particular approach that you should check
with your course tutor.

REVISION NOTE

Remember: when it comes to applying the interpretation after the CJEU has dealt with
the case, it is an issue of EU law that has been discussed. This is where questions on
Article 267 overlap with other areas of *substantive* EU law. The free movement areas,
or competition law, are good examples of where this can be the case. You would need
to bring in your knowledge of these substantive areas alongside the procedure you have
been discussing under Article 267.

Don't be tempted to . . . – This feature
underlines areas where students most often
trip up in exams. Use them to spot common
pitfalls and avoid losing marks.

❗ Don't be tempted to . . .

Article 267 was referred to as Article 177 previously, and then Article 234 under the
Amsterdam renumbering of the Treaty. Cases will refer to the number that was relevant
at the time of the case, and it is therefore important to remember this when reading
the judgments of these cases. You will need to refer to the new Article's number, so be
careful not to get confused. If you cite an old Article number without any reference to the
new numbering, expect to get picked up on it by your examiners.

Read to impress – Focus on these carefully
selected sources to extend your knowledge,
deepen your understanding, and earn better
marks in coursework as well as in exams.

READ TO IMPRESS

Mance, J. (2013) 'The Interface Between National and European Law', 38 EL Rev 437
Saunders, O. (2004) 'A Warning Shot Across the Bows of the ECJ: The Lessons of *Arsenal
   Football Club v Reed*', *Legal Executive Journal* 38
Tridimas, T. (2003) 'Knocking on Heaven's Door: Fragmentation, Efficiency and Defiance in the
   Preliminary Reference Procedure', 40 CMLR 9

Glossary – Forgotten the meaning of a
word? This quick reference covers key
definitions and other useful terms.

Glossary of terms

The glossary is divided into two parts: key definitions and other useful terms. The key
definitions can be found within the chapter in which they occur as well as in the glossary
below. These definitions are the essential terms that you must know and understand in
order to prepare for an exam. The additional list of terms provides further definitions of

Guided tour of the companion website

Book resources are available to download. Print your own **topic maps** and **revision checklists**!

Use the **study plan** prior to your revision to help you assess how well you know the subject and determine which areas need most attention. Choose to take the full assessment or focus on targeted study units.

'Test your knowledge' of individual areas with quizzes tailored specifically to each chapter. **Sample problem and essay questions** are also available with guidance on writing a good answer.

Flashcards test and improve recall of important legal terms, key cases and statutes. Available in both electronic and printable formats.

'You be the marker' gives you the chance to evaluate sample exam answers for different question types and understand how and why an examiner awards marks.

Download the **podcast** and listen as your own personal Law Express tutor guides you through answering a typical but challenging question. A step-by-step explanation on how to approach the question is provided, including what essential elements your answer will need for a pass, how to structure a good response, and what to do to make your answer stand out so that you can earn extra marks.

All of this and more can be found when you visit **www.pearsoned.co.uk/lawexpress**

Table of cases and statutes

UK cases

EU cases

▐ Statutes and EU legislation

■ Directives

■ Regulations

□ REVISION NOTE

The TFEU (commonly referred to as the Treaty of Rome) has been renumbered *twice* now. You need to be aware of this, as otherwise it may become confusing when looking at cases (particularly older ones) which refer to one of the two old numbering systems.

When you are using your textbook, you should see that the book uses the current numbering system (if not, it is likely out-of-date and you should try and use something more recent) but when looking at cases from many years ago, you will still see that the old numbering is referred to. The EU does not go through all the old cases and re-number the Treaty in the judgments, so this table can help you avoid confusion.

From the **1950s** through to the Treaty of Amsterdam (which came into force on **1 May 1999**), the original numbering system was used. Any cases between these times will refer to the original numbers of the Treaty of Rome.

The Amsterdam Treaty renumbered the original Treaty of Rome because with all the amendments that had occurred in over 50 years, the numbering had become untidy and complicated. This was effective from **May 1999** to **December 2009**.

On **1 December 2009,** the Lisbon Treaty renumbered the Treaty of Rome again, for much the same reason.

The table below gives all three versions of the Treaty numbers:

Pre-Amsterdam numbering	Post-Amsterdam numbering	Post-Lisbon numbering
Article 137 EEC	Article 189 EC	Article 14 TEU
Article 5 EEC	Article 10 EC	Article 4(3) TEU
Article 9 EEC	Article 14 EC	Article 28 TFEU
Article 7 EEC	Article 15 EC	Article 29 TFEU
Article 12 EEC	Article 25 EC	Article 30 TFEU
Article 9 EEC	Article 23 EC	Article 31 TFEU
Article 7d EEC	Article 16 EC	Article 32 TFEU
Article 8a EEC	Article 18 EC	Article 33 TFEU
Article 30 EEC	Article 28 EC	Article 34 TFEU
Article 34 EEC	Article 29 EC	Article 35 TFEU
Article 36 EEC	Article 30 EC	Article 36 TFEU ▶

Pre-Amsterdam numbering	Post-Amsterdam numbering	Post-Lisbon numbering
Article 10 EEC	Article 24 EC	Article 37 TFEU
–	–	Article 39 TFEU
Article 57 EEC	Article 47 EC	Article 40 TFEU
Article 48 EEC	Article 39 EC	Article 45 TFEU
Article 49 EEC	Article 40 EC	Article 46 TFEU
Article 73m EEC	Article 65 EC	Article 81 TFEU
Article 85 EEC	Article 81 EC	Article 101 TFEU
Article 86 EEC	Article 82 EC	Article 102 TFEU
Article 138 EEC	Article 190 EC, paras. 4 & 5	Article 223 TFEU
Article 138a EEC	Article 191 EC, second para.	Article 224 TFEU
Article 138b EEC	Article 192 EC, second para.	Article 225 TFEU
Article 138c EEC	Article 193 EC	Article 226 TFEU
Article 138d EEC	Article 194 EC	Article 227 TFEU
Article 138e EEC	Article 195 EC	Article 228 TFEU
Article 139 EEC	Article 196 EC	Article 229 TFEU
Article 140 EEC	Article 197 EC, second, third and fourth paras	Article 230 TFEU
Article 141 EEC	Article 198 EC	Article 231 TFEU
Article 142 EEC	Article 199 EC	Article 232 TFEU
Article 143 EEC	Article 200 EC	Article 233 TFEU
Article 144 EEC	Article 201 EC	Article 234 TFEU
–	–	Article 235 TFEU
–	–	Article 236 TFEU
Article 147 EEC	Article 204 EC	Article 237 TFEU
Article 148 EEC	Article 205 EC, paras. 1 & 3	Article 238 TFEU
Article 150 EEC	Article 206 EC	Article 239 TFEU

Pre-Amsterdam numbering	Post-Amsterdam numbering	Post-Lisbon numbering
Article 151 EEC	Article 207 EC	Article 240 TFEU
Article 152 EEC	Article 208 EC	Article 241 TFEU
Article 153 EEC	Article 209 EC	Article 242 TFEU
Article 154 EEC	Article 210 EC	Article 243 TFEU
–	–	Article 244 TFEU
Article 157 EEC	Article 213 EC	Article 245 TFEU
Article 159 EEC	Article 215 EC	Article 246 TFEU
Article 160 EEC	Article 216 EC	Article 247 TFEU
Article 161 EEC	Article 217 EC, para. 2	Article 248 TFEU
Article 162 EEC	Article 218 EC, para. 2	Article 249 TFEU
Article 163 EEC	Article 219 EC	Article 250 TFEU
Article 169 EEC	Article 226 EC	Article 258 TFEU
Article 170 EEC	Article 227 EC	Article 259 TFEU
Article 171 EEC	Article 228 EC	Article 260 TFEU
Article 173 EEC	Article 230 EC	Article 263 TFEU
Article 175 EEC	Article 232 EC	Article 265 TFEU
Article 177 EEC	Article 234 EC	Article 267 TFEU
Article 185 EEC	Article 242 EC	Article 278 TFEU
Article 186 EEC	Article 243 EC	Article 279 TFEU
Article 189 EEC	Article 249 EC	Article 288 TFEU
–	–	Article 289 TFEU
Article 189b	Article 251 EC	Article 294 TFEU
–	–	Article 15 TEU
–	–	Article 16 TEU
–	–	Article 17 TEU

Sources and application of EU law

1

Revision checklist

Essential points you should know:

☐ Primary and secondary sources of EU law, and how they are created

☐ That EU law is supreme, and must be adhered to, even in the light of contradictory domestic law

☐ The rules of direct applicability and direct effect, and how they affect the ability to enforce EU law in national courts

☐ The principle of state liability for non-implementation of EU law, its consequences for States and individuals, and its link to enforcement proceedings against Member States (see Chapter 3 for details)

☐ How the UK judiciary has applied the above rules, in the light of the constitutional system of the UK

☐ How this affects the rights and duties of individual citizens

■ Topic map

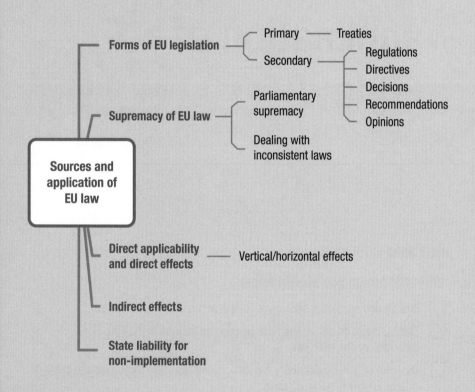

■ Introduction

The operation of the EU is based upon its laws.

These laws are created either through amendments to the Treaties, or through the legislative powers given to the Institutions (see Chapter 2) and are enforceable in the countries of the EU, and in some circumstances are enforceable against citizens of those Member States (see the discussion of Direct Effects below).

The purpose of this chapter is to examine the sources of EU law, and to discuss the system under which they are enforceable. To this end, there are several main issues:

- The supremacy of EU law in Member States' jurisdictions
- The enforceability of those laws directly by individuals in national courts
- The difference between the ways in which those laws are treated.

The EU is pretty unusual in international law. Normally it is very difficult to enforce laws upon signatory States of international agreements; however, the EU has built up a significant body of legislation and case law, referred to as the *acquis communitaire* – basically the existing law of the Community. States can be held to account for non-implementation (this is dealt with in Chapter 3) and individuals in certain situations can directly enforce rights given to them under EU law.

ASSESSMENT ADVICE

This area is very broad, and therefore there is a wide range of assessment questions which could be asked regarding sources of law. These may range from problem questions concerning direct effects through to essay questions on the supremacy of EU law. All these questions have one thing in common – they concern the way in which EU law affects the law of Member States; in particular, the UK.

This is an area of law that has been developed through the case law. It is very important to make sure you are familiar with the key cases that have developed the law here. Examiners will not mark you very highly if you cannot demonstrate a good knowledge of relevant key cases: this chapter will highlight a lot of them. In addition, you should bear in mind that this area is not just about reiterating facts, but that you should be mindful that your examiner will most likely be looking for analysis too.

■ Sample question

Could you answer this question? Below is a typical essay question that could arise on this topic. Guidelines on answering the question are included at the end of this chapter, whilst a sample problem question and guidance on tackling it can be found on the companion website.

ESSAY QUESTION

'It is true that by Article 189 [then 249, now Art. 288] regulations are directly applicable and may therefore certainly produce direct effects by virtue of their nature as law. However, it does not follow from this that other categories of legal measures mentioned in that Article could never produce similar effects.'

Case 9/70 *Franz Grad* v *Finanzamt Traustein* [1970] ECR 825 at 837

Discuss.

■ Forms of EU legislation

EU law falls broadly into two categories, **primary legislation** and **secondary legislation**:

- Primary legislation comes from the Treaties.
- Secondary legislation comes from the law-making powers given to the Institutions under Article 288 TFEU.

Limited competence of EU law

One thing to remember about the EU is that it has what is referred to as 'limited competence'. This means that there are only some areas of law that have been passed onto the EU through the Treaties by the Member States. All other areas are still governed by the Member States themselves. This is important to remember when considering the types of legislation, and also the effect that legislation at EU level has upon the supremacy of EU law.

Primary legislation

> **! Don't be tempted to . . .**
>
> Take care not to confuse the different Treaties with each other. There is now a range of Treaties that affect EU law. However, their place is easy to understand, as follows:
>
> - The Treaty of Rome is the founding Treaty of the European Economic Community (now European Union) and is the main Treaty to refer to. Where this book refers to 'the Treaty', then it is this Treaty which is meant. The Treaty of Lisbon has changed the name of this Treaty, and it is now referred to as the Treaty on the Functioning of the European Union (TFEU).
>
> - The Single European Act, Maastricht Treaty (Treaty on European Union), Amsterdam Treaty, Treaty of Nice and Lisbon Treaty have all amended the Treaty of Rome, and therefore usually you will not need to refer to them directly (with the exception of the Maastricht Treaty which was a more significant amendment than others). Any changes these Treaties have made are included in the most up-to-date version of the Treaty of Rome on the Europa website: http://europa.eu/.
>
> - Bear in mind that the Treaty on European Union (TEU) has now been given greater significance by the changes made by the Lisbon Treaty, and therefore the TFEU is no longer the only Treaty to which you will commonly need to refer.

The order of the Treaties is given in the following table.

Signed	In force from	Treaty
1957	1 January 1958	Treaty of Rome – Treaty on the Functioning of the European Union (TFEU)
1986	1 July 1987	Single European Act
1992	1 November 1993	Treaty of Maastricht – Treaty on European Union (TEU)
1997	1 May 1999	Treaty of Amsterdam
1999	1 February 2003	Treaty of Nice
2007	1 December 2009	Treaty of Lisbon

Primary legislation is only made when Member States meet and agree amendments; usually at intergovernmental conferences. The laws contained in Treaties cannot be changed in any other way, and must do so with the agreement of all Member States.

This is why often there is a considerable delay before a Treaty comes into force – each Member State must ratify the Treaty through their own domestic processes (sometimes requiring a referendum). The Lisbon Treaty demonstrates the political problems that can be encountered when bringing out a new Treaty.

The Constitutional Treaty is not included in this list because it was never completely ratified. France and Holland voted against this Treaty in referenda held after its signature in 2004, and so it never became part of EU law. It can be referred to as an example of EU reform that did not work, however. It is also worth noting that a lot of the content of this Treaty was then transferred to the Treaty of Lisbon and has subsequently become part of EU law – for example, the office of President of the European Council.

Secondary legislation

Secondary legislation is made by the Institutions under the powers given to them by Article 288.

KEY STATUTE

Article 288(1) TFEU

To exercise the Union's competences, the institutions shall adopt regulations, directives, decisions, recommendations and opinions.

The five different forms of secondary legislation can be defined as follows:

Form of legislation	Effect
Regulations (Article 288(2))	Generally applicable – automatically become law in all Member States
Directives (Article 288(3))	Applicable to all Member States, but require some form of enabling legislation from national parliaments of Member States
Decisions (Article 288(4))	Binding only on those parties to whom they are addressed
Recommendations and Opinions (Article 288(5))	Non-binding Acts

■ Supremacy of EU law

Nowhere in the Treaties themselves is there any reference to the supremacy of EU law, or its hierarchy with the national laws of the Member States. Instead, this principle has evolved from case law of the European Court of Justice (ECJ), now renamed the Court of Justice of the European Union (CJEU).

KEY CASE

Case 6/64 *Costa* v *ENEL* [1964] ECR 585

Concerning: Supremacy of EU law

Facts

This case concerned a conflict between several Treaty provisions and an Italian statute which nationalised the electricity company in Italy.

Legal principle

The ECJ said: 'By creating a Community of unlimited duration, having its own institutions, its own personality, its own legal capacity and capacity of representation on the international plane and, more particularly, real powers stemming from a limitation of sovereignty or a transfer of powers from the States of the Community [i.e. Union], the Member States have limited their sovereign rights, albeit within limited fields, and have thus created a body of law which binds both their nationals and themselves.' This therefore established that the Member States had agreed to prioritise EU law above their own within certain areas.

This was also followed by Case 11/70 *International Handelsgesellschaft mbH* [1970] ECR 1125, which went further than *Costa* v *ENEL* by stating that even secondary EU law (in that case a Regulation) was a higher form of law than the constitutional law of a Member State, which has higher status in a national legal system than ordinary statutes. Although this would not affect the UK, as currently there is no written constitution, it does have significance in most of the other EU Member States, as they do. However, the general principle that flows from this does affect the UK – the overall point is that EU law is considered more important than *any* national law, including law made by judges.

When a Member State joins the EU, it effectively agrees to be bound by its laws (as confirmed by *Costa* v *ENEL*, above), both primary and secondary. In particular, Article 4(3) TEU imposes a general obligation on all Member States to make sure they fulfill all obligations under the Treaty. (Until the Lisbon amendments, this was Article 10 of the Treaty of Rome.) This created a problem with the UK constitutional system when the UK joined in 1972, as the UK system is **dualist**.

KEY DEFINITION: Dualist

A legal system where any international agreements signed by that State's government can only become law when legislation is enacted in that country to ratify that agreement. This is common in systems where the parliament is supreme, like the UK constitutional system. This is the opposite of monist systems, where any international agreement automatically becomes part of that State's law merely because the government has signed it.

The doctrine of parliamentary supremacy

The doctrine of parliamentary supremacy (in theory) creates problems, because it states that:

■ Parliament is the highest law-making body in the UK;

■ no other law can override the wishes of Parliament;

■ Parliament cannot bind its successors;

■ any later Act of Parliament which contradicts an earlier one impliedly repeals that law.

The first of these issues was addressed because when the UK joined the EU (at that time the EEC), Parliament enacted the European Communities Act 1972.

KEY STATUTE

European Communities Act 1972, s. 2(1)

All rights, powers, liabilities, obligations and restrictions . . . arising . . . under . . . the Treaties are without further enactment to be given legal effect or used in the United Kingdom and shall be recognised and available in law, and be enforced, allowed and followed accordingly . . .

Therefore, the EU Treaties are recognised as part of UK law because of the European Communities Act, and so this should deal with the issue created by the doctrine of parliamentary supremacy. The thing to note specifically from this case is that the Treaties are adopted into UK law 'without further enactment' and therefore this deals with all other Treaties that may be ratified by the UK as well. What it didn't do was deal with the other three bullet points above, concerning overriding laws, binding successors and implied repeal. These issues were debated in the courts shortly after the UK joined the EU. It created uncertainty at the time, because the judiciary was unused to having to deal with EU law as well as UK law. The rules that evolved at that time have therefore established how the UK courts deal with EU laws.

Dealing with inconsistent laws

Joining the EU therefore had two consequences for the UK:

■ Any existing national laws inconsistent with EU laws had to be repealed.

■ The Member State (in this case the UK) cannot enact laws in the future which are inconsistent with EU law.

The first of these was probably more straightforward to deal with, as the enactment of the European Communities Act could be seen as an indication from Parliament that it agreed to remove previous inconsistent laws. The second consequence was more difficult to deal with.

First, let's look at why EU law was regarded as supreme. The Treaty itself does not make any mention about EU law being supreme, but this is an issue which has been discussed repeatedly by the CJEU (formerly ECJ), and the *Costa* case mentioned above is probably the best example. Also, in Case 26/62 *Van Gend en Loos* v *Nederlandse Administratie der Belastingen* [1963] ECR 1, the ECJ said: '. . . the Community constitutes a new legal order in international law, for whose benefit the States have limited their sovereign rights . . .' and therefore limited their ability to make laws which go against the Treaty. The significance of this was discussed by Lord Denning in the following case.

KEY CASE

Macarthys v *Smith* [1979] 3 All ER 325

Concerning: the effect of the EU Treaty on the application of UK law in the courts

Facts

This case involved a claim by a woman for equal pay with a male counterpart. The Equal Pay Act 1970 would not have given her a remedy, however Article 141 of the EEC Treaty (now Art. 231 TFEU) would have. The Court had to decide whether the law under the Treaty gave her a right that she could enforce directly.

Legal principle

Lord Denning said:

> In construing our statute, we are entitled to look at the treaty as an aid to its construction: and even more, not only as an aid but as an overriding force. If on close investigation it should appear that our legislation is deficient – or is inconsistent with Community law – by some oversight of our draftsmen – then it is our bounden duty to give priority to Community law.

This is fine where the statute concerned can be reinterpreted, and this in fact forms the basis of indirect effect (see later in this chapter for details) but the principle here was properly tested in the next case, where there appeared to have been a deliberate attempt to go against EU law by enacting a conflicting UK law.

As a consequence, the European Communities Act appears to give the TFEU a kind of higher status. This is implied in the situation set by the cases the idea that, no matter what UK law is inconsistent with EU law, the Treaty will still have priority.

KEY CASE

R v Secretary of State for Transport, ex parte Factortame (No. 2) [1990] 3 CMLR 1
Concerning: supremacy of EU law and conflicting national law

Facts

A dispute arose over the Merchant Shipping Act 1988, which attempted to restrict ownership of UK registered fishing boats by requiring that at least 75 per cent of each boat must be owned by UK nationals. The courts had to decide, as there was a direct conflict between the Merchant Shipping Act and the EC Treaty, which should be applied.

Legal principle

After referring this to the ECJ (now the CJEU) for clarification, the House of Lords (now the Supreme Court) decided that, where there is conflict between a national law and Community law, the doctrine of parliamentary supremacy is modified by section 2(4) of the European Communities Act 1972, and allowed the House of Lords to disregard the Merchant Shipping Act, something it had never been able to do before. In this case, this allowed the Spanish fishermen who complained to the courts to get interim relief, and eventually led to the relevant parts of the Merchant Shipping Act being repealed.

It is important to point out that this is the case *regardless of whether the Act in question came before or after the European Communities Act.*

■ Direct applicability and direct effects

So EU law is supreme; however, when applying it to real situations (as, for example, when you are asked to apply the law to problem-based scenarios), then you also need to be able to show whether it can be directly used or not. This is where the concepts of direct applicability and direct effects come in. Being able to use these concepts will enable you to say whether someone can use an EU law in their national court or not.

! Don't be tempted to . . .

There is often confusion between the terms *direct applicability* and *direct effect*. It is important not to get these two concepts mixed up as they are quite different. As a general definition, you can think of the two as follows:

Direct applicability: EU law is directly applicable if it is recognised as part of UK law. Treaties and Regulations are directly applicable because they become part of UK law as a result of the European Communities Act 1972. Directives are not directly applicable as they need an implementing piece of UK legislation to become law in the UK.

Directly effective: EU law is directly effective if it can be enforced in a UK court. There are two types of direct effects, horizontal and vertical. The difference between these is explained further below.

Linked to the issue of supremacy of EU law is the question of directly enforcing EU law in national courts. The above discussion has shown that EU law overrides UK law, but this is meaningless unless a person can enforce those laws in a UK court. However, in certain circumstances, EU law has been held to be directly enforceable in national courts through the doctrine of direct effect. This was first raised in the following key case.

KEY CASE

Case 26/62 *Van Gend en Loos* v *Nederlandse Administratie der Belastingen* [1963] ECR 1

Concerning: direct effect of EU law in national courts

Facts

This case concerned Article 30 (at that time Art. 12, then subsequently Art. 25 pre-Lisbon) of the TFEU which prohibited new customs duties being imposed, or existing customs duties being increased. Through a case in the Dutch courts, Van Gend was trying to directly enforce the rule in Article 30 against the Dutch government, claiming it gave them a right not to be taxed in this way. The question was referred to the ECJ (now the CJEU) under Article 267 TFEU (at that time Art. 177).

Legal principle

Although Article 30 was a prohibition, the ECJ (now the CJEU) said that Van Gend could enforce this against the Dutch government if the following criteria were fulfilled:

- that it was a clear and unconditional prohibition;
- that it imposed a duty without any discretion given to the Member States;
- that it produced direct effects between Member States and citizens.

As these criteria were fulfilled in this case, then the national court could enforce Article 30 in favour of Van Gend.

KEY CASE

Case 41/74 *Van Duyn* v *Home Office* [1974] ECR 1337

Concerning: criteria for establishing whether a provision of EU law has direct effect

Facts

The UK government was attempting to exclude Van Duyn, a Dutch national, from the UK because of her membership of an 'undesirable' organisation, the Church of Scientology. Part of this case looked at whether Directive 64/221/EEC could be directly enforced by Van Duyn.

Legal principle

In order for a provision of EU law to have direct effects, it must:

- be clear and precise;
- be unconditional/without exceptions;
- not require any implementation by the Member States.

These cases clearly established that it was possible for an individual to enforce a rule of EU law, without having to rely upon a national rule, despite the fact that this was usually required as Directives are specifically implemented individually by the Member States. The application of this rule, however, will be different according to the different type of EU Act being enforced. Treaties and Regulations are directly applicable and directly effective, but Directives are not directly applicable, and are only directly **effective vertically**.

Vertical and horizontal effect

KEY DEFINITION: Vertical and horizontal effect

An EU law is **vertically effective** when it is enforceable only against the State. It is **horizontally effective** when it is enforceable against private individuals (people and companies) as well as against the State.

Type of EU law	Vertically/horizontally effective?
Treaties	Can be both vertically and **horizontally effective**, depending on the nature of the right being given by the Treaty article – you need to refer to *Van Gend en Loos*
Regulations	Can be both vertically and horizontally effective

Type of EU law	Vertically/horizontally effective?
Directives	Vertically effective only – a Directive is an instruction to a Member State to introduce a law into its own legal system
Decisions	Decisions are addressed to particular parties – so they are enforceable only against those parties

The problem of direct effect of Directives

This is the part of direct effect that students struggle with most – directly enforcing a Directive in a national court causes the most problems because of the nature of a Directive. Directives are instructions to the Member States to enact a law, and therefore they are only capable of having vertical effect. The main thing to note is that Directives do not *automatically* have direct effects, and so if a person wants to enforce them in a national court, they must make sure the following conditions apply.

Condition	Case example
The Directive must give clearly identifiable rights to individuals	Case 43/75 *Defrenne* v *SABENA (No. 2)* [1979] ECR 1365
The time limit for the Member State to implement the Directive must have passed	Case 148/78 *Pubblico Ministero* v *Ratti* [1979] ECR 1629
The Directive can be enforced only against the State (vertically)	Case 152/84 *Marshall* v *Southampton & South West Hampshire Area Health Authority* [1986] ECR 723

! Don't be tempted to . . .

One area where the CJEU has been flexible with its definition concerns the meaning of 'the State' under the vertical effects rule. This is an area where students can be caught out when dealing with a problem question which involves vertical effect. Look at these three examples:

■ In Case C-188/89 *Foster* v *British Gas* [1990] ECR I-3313 the ECJ (now the CJEU) said that a body would be part of the State if it:

☐ is subject to the control of the State;

☐ has special powers given to it by the State. ▶

- Case 152/84 *Marshall* v *Southampton & South West Hampshire Area Health Authority* [1986] ECR 723 shows that 'the State' is 'the State' regardless of what function it is performing (in *Marshall* it was acting as an employer).

- In *NUT* v *Governing Body of St. Mary's Church of England (Aided) Junior School* [1997] 3 CMLR 630 the court decided that the definition of 'the State' should be a 'broad one'. Schools and other educational establishments would therefore be part of 'the State'.

When thinking about whether something is part of 'the State', it is important to bear in mind this broad definition – but there are limits: see *Rolls Royce* v *Doughty* [1992] ICR 538 where, although Rolls Royce were publicly owned, they were not part of 'the State' as they did not fulfil the other criteria associated with being part of 'the State' (see above).

■ Other ways of enforcing EU law in national courts

Indirect effect

When EU law imposes an obligation on 'the State', the definition is very broad, and therefore also includes the courts as well. This has led to the CJEU finding that the courts also have an obligation to interpret national law in line with EU law.

KEY CASE

Case 14/83 *von Colson* v *Land Nordrhein-Westfalen* [1984] ECR 1891

Concerning: indirect effect of Community law

Facts

This case involved two female social workers who were attempting to claim rights under the Equal Treatment Directive. They could not claim rights directly under the Directive, however the ECJ (now the CJEU) decided that the Directive could still be useful through what became indirect effect.

Legal principle

The ECJ (CJEU) developed what is often referred to as the 'von Colson principle': that as national courts are part of the State, they are under an obligation to interpret national law in line with EU law. This can mean that an individual can enforce a law from the EU against another individual in a national court.

This appears to solve all problems created by the limits of direct effects (particularly with Directives, because they can only have vertical effects), but if you look at Case C-106/89 *Marleasing* v *La Comercial Internacional de Alimentación* [1990] ECR I-4135, it is important that a national law *exists* that can be interpreted.

Below is an example of how it has been dealt with by judges in the UK.

KEY CASE

Litster v *Forth Dry Dock* [1989] 2 WLR 634

Concerning: the application of indirect effect in the UK

Facts

This concerned Directive 77/187/EEC, which was intended to protect workers who were dismissed as a result of a transfer of a business. The UK statutory instrument that enacted it required that workers dismissed immediately before the transfer should be protected. The employees in question were dismissed one hour before the transfer, and so on a literal interpretation were not employed immediately before the transfer.

Legal principle

The House of Lords (now the Supreme Court) decided that they had to construe the UK Regulations in such a way that it 'accords with the decisions of the European Court upon the corresponding provisions of the Directive to which the Regulation was intended to give effect'. They interpreted the Regulations so that those employees dismissed one hour before transfer were protected, as this was consistent with the wording of the Directive.

State liability for non-implementation

There is one final method of gaining a remedy based on EU law – to sue the State because of its failure to implement a piece of legislation where it was obliged to do so. This is *mainly* relevant to Directives, because they normally need a national law to give effect to them, but not exclusively.

KEY CASE

Cases C-6 & 9/90 *Francovich* v *Italy* [1991] ECR I-5357

Concerning: state liability for failing to implement a Directive

Facts

This case concerned employees of a bankrupt company who were trying to claim wages arrears, something which was guaranteed by a Directive which Italy had failed to implement. Because they could not sue their former employer (because that would have involved a horizontal effect, not possible with a Directive) they then sued the Italian State, claiming that it was at fault because they could not get a remedy. ▶

Legal principle

The ECJ (now the CJEU) held that the Italian State would be liable for its failure to implement the Directive if the following three conditions were fulfilled:

- the Directive gave rights to individuals;
- those rights were identifiable within the wording of the Directive; and
- there was a causal link between the failure to implement and the damage caused to the individual.

This has now been applied to all forms of EU law (see Cases C-46 & 48/93 *Brasserie du Pecheur* v *Germany* and *R* v *Secretary of State for Transport, ex parte Factortame* [1996] ECR I-1029). These cases also added the requirement that the breach must be 'sufficiently serious' in order to be able to apply this principle to all forms of EU law. The joined cases of C-178–179/94 & 188–190/94 *Dillenkofer* v *Republic of Germany* [1996] ECR I-4845 also established that the failure to correctly implement a Directive was automatically considered to be 'sufficiently serious'. This therefore indicated the importance of Directives as part of the *acquis communitaire*.

! Don't be tempted to . . .

An area where enforcement of Directives in problem questions causes issues concerns against whom precisely you are taking action. Students in the past have been confused about who is being sued in action under direct effects/State liability, where a body is counted as being part of, or an 'emanation' of the State. The temptation is just to assume that you sue the State directly, therefore, central government. But, bear in mind:

- Where a person is using direct effect, they are suing the body or organisation responsible for their problem, e.g. in *Marshall* and in *Foster*, these individuals were suing the local health authority and British Gas respectively.
- Where a person is using State liability, they are suing the State as an entity, so in *Francovich*, they were suing the Italian State.

✓ Make your answer stand out

A more controversial aspect of State liability has been the idea that the State could be liable for the actions of the judiciary. This does fit in with the broader concept of 'the State' as discussed by the CJEU. This is controversial because the State does not have any control or influence over the judiciary. If you encounter a question where the judiciary is breaching EU law, or is required to fulfil obligations under Article 4(3) TEU, then you might consider this point. See Anagnostaras (2001).

The problem of non-implementation of Directives and the post-Lisbon solution

Many problems have been encountered in the past where a State has failed to implement a Directive and therefore an individual has not been able to get a remedy. This is where the rule of vertical effect for Directives creates an unfair split between the public and the private sectors, because although those in the public sector may be able to argue that they are suing an 'emanation of the State' under the principles in *Foster* v *British Gas*, those who may need to enforce Directives against private bodies will be unfairly prejudiced. A mechanism to minimise this is in the new Article 260 (formerly 228). The Commission can recommend a fine the *first* time the matter goes to the CJEU when the infringement by the State is about failing to comply with EU law, and not have to wait for a second action. The aim is to deter States from attempting to use the long Article 258 procedure to avoid enacting Directives.

■ Putting it all together

Answer guidelines

See the essay question at the start of the chapter.

Approaching the question

This question is focused upon the principle of direct effect discussed in part of this chapter, but it is also broad enough to enable you to bring in other areas of this topic from this chapter. You need to discuss Article 288 and the way that direct effect has affected the application of the types of laws discussed. So this is essentially about how enforceable EU rules are in national court systems, and you will therefore need to bear this in mind in the way that you construct your answer. The question has picked out Regulations as being subject to really straightforward rules regarding direct effect, but that other forms of legislation are affected by this principle also. So a generally sensible approach would involve discussing direct effects in the context of other forms of *binding* legislation under Article 288, Directives and Decisions, as well as Treaty Articles.
▶

Important points to include

In your answer, you will need to address the following:

- The distinction between direct applicability and direct effect.
- The different rules for direct applicability/effect of Treaties, Regulations, Directives, Decisions.
- A discussion of how the rules have been applied by the courts to these different forms of legislation; in particular, the way in which rules concerning Directives have evolved.
- How these rules can, in certain situations, provide solutions to members of the public.
- How the shortcomings of direct effect of Directives (lack of horizontal effect) have been addressed through use of indirect effect and state liability for non-implementation.
- How the use of state liability for non-implementation should only be considered once the other avenues have been exhausted.

 Make your answer stand out

This question is asking you to explain the operation of the rules of direct applicability/effect to forms of legislation other than Regulations, and the most complicated of these is Directives. Directives create problems because of the nature of what they are: instructions to Member States. The binding nature of Directives therefore applies to only the State or bodies that can be said to be emanations of the State. Therefore, if you can show your appreciation of the limitations of Directives, and how the courts have developed rules to deal with this (for example, the broad definition of 'the State' discussed above), as well as the limitations still in existence (the difference between employees in the public and in the private sectors under the rules in *Marshall*, for example), then you can demonstrate an understanding of how these rules work in practice.

READ TO IMPRESS

Anagnostaras, G. (2001) 'The Principle of State Liability for Judicial Breaches: The Impact of European Community Law', 7 EPL 281

Craig, P. (1991) 'Sovereignty of the United Kingdom Parliament after *Factortame*', 9 YEL 221

Craig, P. (1997) 'Directives: Direct Effect, Indirect Effect and the Construction of National Legislation', 22 EL Rev 519

Craig, P. (1997) 'Once More Unto the Breach: The Community, the State and Damages Liability', 113 LQR 67

Steiner, J. (1993) 'From Direct Effects to Francovich: Shifting Means of Enforcement of Community Law', 18 EL Rev 3

Tridimas, T. (2002) 'Black, White, and Shades of Grey: Horizontality of Directives Revisited', 21 YEL 327

www.pearsoned.co.uk/lawexpress

 Go online to access more revision support including quizzes to test your knowledge, sample questions with answer guidelines, podcasts you can download, and more!

The Institutions
of the EU and the
decision-making
process

2

Revision checklist

Essential points you should know:

☐ The structure of the EU Institutions and how they relate to each other

☐ The role of each of the Institutions, and their powers and duties

☐ How the above affects both the political and legal life of the Community, and the implications of the exercise of those powers by the Institutions

■ Topic map

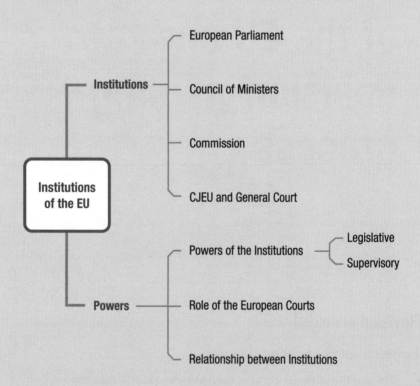

■ Introduction

The EU is run by its Institutions.

The key to understanding the way in which the EU operates, therefore, lies in understanding the functions of the Institutions. The EU has two very important roles which have a very real effect on the Member States. First, it makes law, whether that be through Treaties or secondary legislation, and, secondly, it provides adjudication on those laws applicable to all Member States. Each of the Institutions has a key role in achieving these functions, and their powers and their interrelationships are important in showing how this works. The functions and powers of the Institutions tend not to contribute to their own discrete question in an examination, as something focused purely on the mechanics of how the Institutions do things would present a topic purely descriptive in nature. However, an analysis of the politics of how the Institutions work and the political context in which EU law operates can form part of a question in this area. It also helps to understand the Institutions for other topics such as the legislative process itself, and the actions of the three main Institutions when appearing in front of the CJEU. This is why this chapter covers both of these areas which, you may have noticed, are dealt with separately in most textbooks. There is often one chapter describing the Institutions, and one describing their roles and powers. However, we are going to examine the relationships between the Institutions alongside the information about what they are, in order to understand how the powers of each Institution interrelate, and in order for you to understand how this information is relevant and applicable in an examination situation.

One further thing to bear in mind – with the reforms from the Lisbon Treaty, the Institutional structure is one thing which has changed in such a way that it affects how you analyse the relationships between the Institutions. You therefore need to be careful about using out-of-date information and older textbooks. For example, the European Council now has status as a Treaty Institution, which it didn't have before, and there are now new roles within the institutional structure, such as the President of the EU.

ASSESSMENT ADVICE

Essay questions

Questions in this area will commonly focus on some aspect of the relationship between two or more of the Institutions. Such questions will usually require you to have the knowledge of the functions of the Institutions, but will also require you to use that ▶

knowledge to analyse the relationships between the Institutions concerned. So you must remember that this is not an exercise in just memorising large quantities of factual information, you will be required to do something with that information, and it will require some form of critique on your part.

Problem questions

Questions covering this area will generally be ones which overlap with other areas of EU law, for example relating to an aspect of an Institution's powers, like the Commission's power of enforcement under Article 258 TFEU. You will need to understand how the Institutions work in order to advise how the procedures might affect your answer to the question. However, that is not to say that the constitution of an institution is always going to affect the procedure, so you need to make sure you only stick to what is relevant; for example, the role of the Commissioners in the European Commission isn't relevant to your discussion of the Commission's use of the enforcement procedure under Article 258.

■ Sample question

Could you answer this question? Below is a typical essay question that could arise on this topic. Guidelines on answering the question are included at the end of this chapter, whilst a sample problem question and guidance on tackling it can be found on the companion website.

ESSAY QUESTION

'. . . it has become common to speak of an "institutional balance" within Community institutions, and the way in which this is evoked draws on a system of checks and balances not dissimilar to those we find in more traditional governmental systems. The EU institutions have come to operate a system of checks on each other, sometimes referred to in the context of an "institutional balance". . .'

Douglass-Scott, S., *Constitutional Law of the European Union*
(Longman, 2002, Chapter 2 at p. 49)

To what extent does the above statement still apply to the current relationship between the Commission, the Council of Ministers, the European Council and the European Parliament since the ratification of the Lisbon Treaty, particularly as regards maintaining the balance of interests between the European Union and the Member States?

■ The Institutions of the EU

The three primary *legislative* Institutions (Figure 2.1) exist to represent different parties in the EU:

- the Council of Ministers represents the interests of the Member States' governments;
- the European Parliament serves the interests of the EU citizens; and
- the Commission's role is to serve the interests of the EU as an organisation.

Additionally, the Court of Justice of the European Union (CJEU) and the General Court (formerly CFI) are there to adjudicate on cases arising from the Treaty, and there are also other Institutions which serve in an advisory or consultative role, such as the Economic and Social Committee, or the Committee of the Regions. The European Council is also now officially recognised as an Institution of the EU, since the Lisbon Treaty. Its official recognition has had an effect upon the roles of the other Institutions, although it does not participate in making legislation.

! Don't be tempted to . . .

With the passing of the Lisbon Treaty, the European Court of Justice (ECJ) was renamed the Court of Justice of the European Union (CJEU). You may notice in your textbooks that some still refer to it under its old name, but increasingly authors are adopting the new name. Although this may seem like a minor point, make sure you use the proper name, as this will show you are aware that this change has taken place. Although it may be tempting, try not to use the old name (ECJ). You will notice that the ECJ is now referred to as the CJEU throughout this text.

Above all, try not to get confused by what is a relatively minor name change.

Figure 2.1

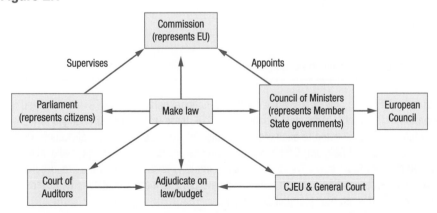

■ Composition of the Institutions

The European Parliament

The European Parliament is constituted of 766 MEPs directly elected by individual citizens of the EU in elections. The number of MEPs allocated to a Member State varies according to population size, with Germany as the State with the largest population size having the largest number of MEPs (99) and Malta, as the State with the smallest population, having just 6. The division is criticised because it is not even – a German MEP will represent a larger number of citizens than an MEP from Malta. The exact numbers currently are as follows:

State	No. of MEPs per State
Germany	99
France	74
UK, Italy	73
Spain	54
Poland	51
Romania	33
Holland	26
Belgium, Czech Republic, Greece, Hungary, Portugal	22
Sweden	20
Austria	19
Bulgaria	18
Denmark, Finland, Slovakia	13
Ireland, Lithuania, Croatia	12
Latvia	9
Slovenia	8
Cyprus, Estonia, Luxembourg, Malta	6

Currently MEPs are only organised according to national party divisions, and are elected for a period of five years. At the next elections in 2014, there will be further changes to the number of MEPs allocated to each Member State, for example Germany's allocation will be reduced to 96, and Belgium, Czech Republic, Greece, Hungary and Portugal's allocation will be reduced to 21 each. These changes are made to ensure appropriate proportions regarding representation of EU citizens across the EU, and there are likely to be further changes if and when new Member States join.

Why is this important?

The European Parliament is directly elected by the population of the EU. Although the MEPs will inevitably be connected with the national parties in each of the States, they are not an extension of the government there. And as the MEPs come from all the political parties in a particular State, they do not represent the interests of the government of the day. Because of this, they are primarily there to represent the interests of the people in their constituency. They are directly linked to the citizens of the EU.

 Make your answer stand out

The development of the European Parliament from the point that direct elections were introduced is an important theme in EU law. It has a significant effect on the balance between the Institutions, and remembering this will help you in your discussion about the relationships between them. Increasing powers have been given to the European Parliament over the years because it is democratic (at least it is perceived as such as it is the only body where people are directly elected to it), and a direct link to EU citizens. The EU has shown that it believes that increasing its powers addresses the problems of 'democratic deficit' (discussed later in this chapter). It is the Institution whose role has changed and evolved the most during the period that the EU (and previously the EEC) has existed.

The Council of the European Union (commonly, the Council of Ministers)

The Council of Ministers is composed of ministerial representatives of the Member State governments. Each State will send a minister relevant to the matter being debated, and therefore the representative will vary accordingly. There used to be as many as 22 configurations, but this has now been reduced to 9 (listed below). You can see the types of issues covered by discussions in the Council:

- General Affairs and External Relations
- Economic and Financial Affairs
- Competitiveness
- Cooperation in the fields of Justice and Home Affairs
- Transport, Telecommunications and Energy
- Agriculture and Fisheries
- Environment
- Education, Youth and Culture.

Each State has a number of votes, and the votes are weighted in a similar way to the weighting in the European Parliament, although you will see that they are slightly different, for example although Germany has far more MEPs than the UK or Italy, it has exactly the same number of votes in the Council of Ministers.

State	Number of votes in the Council of Ministers
Germany, France, Italy, UK	29
Spain, Poland	27
Romania	14
Holland	13
Belgium, Czech Republic, Greece, Hungary, Portugal	12
Austria, Bulgaria, Sweden	10
Croatia, Denmark, Ireland, Lithuania, Slovakia, Finland	7
Estonia, Cyprus, Latvia, Luxembourg, Slovenia	4
Malta	3

This makes a total of 352 votes. The Council of Ministers will vote either by **qualified majority voting**, bare majority, or unanimity.

KEY DEFINITION: Qualified majority voting

Qualified majority voting (QMV) requires the following:

- a minimum of 260 out of 352 votes cast in favour;
- a majority of all Member States voting in favour;
- at least 62 per cent of the EU's total population represented by the vote in favour.

Voting can be a complicated and highly political issue. Type in the following link in your computer's web browser to go to the EU's own 'Voting Calculator' at http://ue.eu.int/council/voting-calculator?lang=en

Presidency of the Council of Ministers

Under the previous system, the Presidency of the Council of Ministers was held by each of the Member States in turn, for a period of six months. During that time, the State which held the Presidency put forward proposals and reforms that it wanted to implement, and proposed policies it favoured. The head of government for that State represented the State as President of the Council of Ministers. Prior to the introduction of the Lisbon Treaty, the Presidency was seen as significant in terms of the strategic discussions on the policies of the EU by heads of state of Member countries, and this was mainly because the Presidency of the Council of Ministers also controlled the Presidency of the European Council. However, this is now replaced under the Lisbon reforms with 'team presidencies', and each of the configurations listed above would have a Member State in charge, with the exception of the Foreign Affairs configuration, which is chaired by the High Representative for Foreign Affairs. These would be rotated in the same way as before.

> **! Don't be tempted to . . .**
>
> With the introduction of the Lisbon Treaty in December 2009, the European Council is now an official Institution of the EU. However, it is important not to confuse it with the Council of Ministers, as they have very different roles to play. The European Council arose from unofficial meetings of the heads of state of the Member States, and its main purpose is to discuss the policy direction of the EU. The Council of Ministers is far more focused on the implementation of those policies.

European Council

The European Council is now an official Institution of the EU. It is easily confused with the Council of Ministers, as they are both made up of representatives of national governments. However, each has a different role to play. Put simply:

- The Council of Ministers' role is broadly stated, under Article 16 TEU, to coordinate the economic policies of the Member States, and to take decisions. They are involved in making legislation and in the running of the EU. Their powers can also be found in Articles 237–243 TFEU.

- The European Council's responsibilities are described in Article 15 TEU as being to 'provide the Union with the necessary impetus for its development and shall define the general political directions and priorities thereof. It shall not exercise legislative functions'.

The President of the European Council

The Lisbon Treaty has introduced a new office – that of President of the European Council. This office replaces the revolving six-monthly presidency system previously operated, and is a post elected by qualified majority of the Member States (see Art. 15(5) and (6) TEU). The office runs for two and a half years, and can only be renewed once. In December 2009, the first President of the European Council was appointed, Herman Van Rumpuy. Before taking this office, he had been the Belgian Prime Minister. At the time of writing, he is still the President, as he was re-elected by the Member States for a second term, but as this term is due to expire in December 2014, he will be replaced by a successor as the President is only permitted to serve two terms of office. The overall responsibility of the President is contained in Article 15(6) TEU:

KEY STATUTE

Article 15(6) TEU

The President of the European Council:

(a) shall chair it and drive forward its work;

(b) shall ensure the preparation and continuity of the work of the European Council in cooperation with the President of the Commission, and on the basis of the work of the General Affairs Council;

(c) shall endeavour to facilitate cohesion and consensus within the European Council;

(d) shall present a report to the European Parliament after each of the meetings of the European Council.

The President of the European Council shall, at his level and in that capacity, ensure the external representation of the Union on issues concerning its common foreign and security policy, without prejudice to the powers of the High Representative of the Union for Foreign Affairs and Security Policy.

The President of the European Council shall not hold a national office.

An important point to remember about the President of the European Council is that his role is not about making final decisions himself – in this way he differs from our traditional ideas of a president, for example the President of the United States of America. The President of the European Council is there to facilitate decision-making in meetings involving the Member States, and so the job of making those decisions still lies with the Member States.

✎ EXAM TIP

The office of President of the European Council, along with the post of High Representative for Foreign Affairs and Security Policy and the recognition of the European Council as a Treaty Institution, marks a significant change in the structure of the EU. If you encounter a question which asks you to comment on these developments, or generally about the direction of the EU (for example, an examiner might ask a general question about federalism), then you should be critically reviewing these developments as part of your answer.

European Commission

The European Commission consists of one appointed Commissioner from each State. This is due to change with the next Commission, with a rota system coming into place whereby Member States will take turns to nominate Commissioners. This is because, as the number of Member States has grown, the number of Commissioners has grown, and it has been recognised that the Commission does not need 28 Commissioners.

Each Commissioner will represent a different area of the Commission's business, for example trade and industry or the environment, known as a portfolio. They will also be supported by Directorates General. The President of the Commission is nominated from the list of Commissioners, and this person will also choose a number of Vice-Presidents – although there is theoretically no limit to the number that can be appointed.

✎ EXAM TIP

Where examination questions focus upon the Institutions, you should not use this as an opportunity merely to regurgitate facts about their composition and powers. The study of the Institutions is as much about the intricacies of how they allow the EU to function as it is about their powers. For example, the fact that the Commission is constituted of a representative of each State goes a long way towards helping the Member States to feel involved in policy-making, and to accept policies coming out of the Commission, despite the fact that Commissioners are persons 'whose independence is beyond doubt' – Article 245 TFEU.

The Court of Justice of the European Union and the General Court

📖 REVISION NOTE

Although it is important to know what the CJEU and the General Court are, you will tend to find assessment questions will more readily concentrate on what they *do*, and how this affects the operation of the EU. For example, see the Article 267 reference procedure (Chapter 5), or the contentious procedures that take place in the CJEU and the General Court (Chapters 3 and 4).

❗ Don't be tempted to . . .

Don't confuse the courts of the EU with any other 'European' courts. Remember when European courts are mentioned here, that these are the EU's own courts, and they are given the role of dealing with the laws of the EU. You should not, for example, confuse the Court of Justice of the European Union (CJEU) with the European Court of Human Rights (ECtHR) as this is an entirely separate court, dealing with entirely different matters, and not part of the EU structure.

Other Institutions

There are also several other Institutions involved in the day-to-day processes of the EU, shown in the following table.

Institution	Role	Personnel
Economic and Social Committee	To be consulted by the Council and Commission on legislative proposals Can also submit its own opinion on European matters without being asked	Representatives of various groups concerned with economic activities, such as manufacturers, farmers, trade unionists, or public interest groups
Committee of the Regions	To be consulted by the Council and Commission on legislative proposals	Representatives of regional interests
Court of Auditors	To control and supervise the implementation of the budget	One member from each of the 27 Member States

■ Powers of the Institutions

The powers of the primary Institutions can be broadly broken down into **legislative and supervisory power**, and it is a combination of these two types of power that helps with the smooth running of the EU.

> **KEY DEFINITION: Legislative and supervisory power**
>
> **Legislative power**: The involvement of an Institution in amending, or agreeing to, legislation made by the EU under the Treaties.
>
> **Supervisory power**: The power of an Institution to monitor, supervise or scrutinise the actions of another Institution in the EU Institutional structure.

Institution	Powers and duties
European Parliament (see Art. 14 TEU and Arts. 223–234 TFEU)	Participates in the legislative process. Supervises the European Commission

Institution	Powers and duties
Council of the European Union (commonly referred to as the Council of Ministers) (see Art. 16 TEU and Arts. 237–243 TFEU)	Makes the final decision on legislative proposals, coordinates economic policies of the Member States, delegates power to other Institutions
European Commission (see Art. 17 TEU and Arts. 244–250 TFEU)	Enforcer of the Treaties. Drafts legislative proposals and initiates policy once formulated by the Council of Ministers
European Council (see Art. 15 TEU and Arts. 235 and 236 TFEU)	Now a Treaty Institution because of the Lisbon amendments. A political Institution that represents the Member States and drives reform in the EU. Does not participate in making legislation
Court of Justice of the European Union (formerly ECJ)	Hears cases directed to it under the Treaty. Hears appeals on points of law from the General Court. Rules on matters of interpretation referred to it by courts of Member States
General Court (formerly CFI)	Hears cases directed to it under the Treaty, including staff cases of the EU

✎ **EXAM TIP**

A key theme when considering the Institutions is the development in the role of the European Parliament, both in legislative power and supervisory power. The European Parliament was previously called the Assembly, and prior to 1979 was constituted of nominated representatives from national parliaments of the Member States.

The introduction of direct elections in 1979 kick-started a process whereby the European Parliament has gradually been given more power and influence within the structure of the EU. This process is motivated by the accusation that there is democratic deficit in the EU. Many of the powers are ones that have been added as a result of different Treaties. See the table below for a breakdown of powers and their introduction.

If you encounter a question in an exam that appears to require you to discuss this issue, make sure you are familiar with the relevant development and powers of the European Parliament, and its relationship with the other Institutions (see later in this chapter).

KEY DEFINITION: Democratic deficit

The 'democratic deficit' is the accusation levelled at the EU that it lacks democracy in its legislative Institutions. Attempts have been made to address this by reform of the European Parliament. It essentially refers to the fact that prior to 1979, none of the Institutions had directly elected members. The Commission is appointed, the Council of Ministers contains elected representatives (but those elected to national office) and the European Parliament is now the only Institution where members are directly elected by citizens of the EU. This change, and the reforms in the powers of the European Parliament, are intended to address the lack of democratic accountability in the EU.

Legislative powers

The Commission, Council of Ministers and Parliament all participate in making legislation, a process which also involves other consultative bodies including the Committee of the Regions and the Economic and Social Committee. A summary of the relationship between the Institutions when making legislation is given in Figure 2.2.

A key theme in this area is the way in which the Parliament's role in making law increased, particularly during the 1980s and 1990s. Traditionally the Parliament had very few powers, because prior to 1979 the MEPs were appointed, rather than elected. Successive amendments to the legislative process have increased the involvement of the Parliament so that now, in some matters, the Parliament is placed on an equal footing with the Council of Ministers. Prior to the Treaty of Lisbon, there was a complex list of procedures to be used, which resulted from amendments in successive Treaties. These are listed in the table below.

Figure 2.2

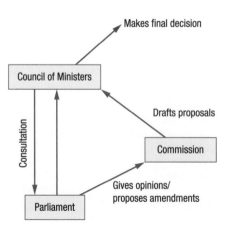

Legislative procedure	Role of the European Parliament
Consultation procedure	Parliament has the right to be consulted
Cooperation procedure (introduced by the Single European Act 1986)	Parliament has the right to be consulted; and Parliament has the right to object to a Council and Commission 'common position' but its objection can be overruled by a unanimous vote in the Council of Ministers
Co-decision procedure (introduced by the Treaty of Maastricht 1992)	Parliament has the right to be consulted; and Parliament has the right to reject a Council and Commission 'common position'; and Parliament has the right to propose amendments. The final decision on the legislative proposal is a 'co-decision' between the Parliament and the Council of Ministers

✎ EXAM TIP

Parliament's involvement in the legislative process has increased with successive Treaty amendments as new legislative procedures have been introduced. If you are ever faced with an exam question which discusses the issue of the increasing involvement of the Parliament in making law, then it is useful to refer to this.

The procedures have now changed, post-Lisbon, as shown in the following table.

Procedure	Description
Ordinary legislative procedure (Art. 294 TFEU)	This is what used to be called the co-decision procedure (above) and is now the default legislative procedure. It involves a joint decision being taken between the Council of Ministers and the Parliament, putting them on an equal footing. If there is no agreement, then a Conciliation Committee is used to negotiate a compromise
Special legislative procedure (Art. 289 TFEU)	This is either a decision of the Parliament with the Council of Ministers' involvement (in which case a joint decision) or a decision of the Council of Ministers with the European Parliament's involvement (in which case it is the same as the old consultation procedure, whereby Parliament has a right to be consulted and put forward its opinion, but the decision is taken by the Council of Ministers)

There is also provision for the Council and Commission to act alone, or the Commission to act alone, in very limited circumstances.

As well as this change in legislative procedures (which has mostly affected the European Parliament's power), the qualified majority voting procedure will be replaced in 2014 by a double majority system.

Increased role of national parliaments

Article 12 TEU now provides for more direct involvement of the national parliaments in the decision-making process at EU level. They are to be most involved in the area of subsidiarity (the process of making sure that EU law is made at the most appropriate level) but also they are now more formally involved in the process of reviewing draft legislation. Before Lisbon this did happen, but to a limited extent, because of the lack of time given to national parliaments and the sheer volume of legislation.

✎ EXAM TIP

This increased role of national parliaments shows a link between this area of EU law and the influence of the EU in UK public law/constitutional law subjects, taught elsewhere in your LL.B degree. An appreciation of this link can therefore show that you understand the wider context within which the EU system operates, and how it affects the sovereignty of national parliaments. This increased role can also help you to demonstrate a link between EU law and democratically elected national parliaments, and therefore be a point to raise regarding democratic deficit, discussed above.

Supervisory powers of the European Parliament

The Institutions of the EU exist in a system whereby certain supervision takes place between the Institutions.

In particular, the Parliament, along with increased legislative powers, now also has the power to supervise the European Commission, and has limited supervisory powers over the Council of Ministers.

- The Parliament has the right to approve the appointment of the President of the Commission and the Commissioners (Art. 17(7) TEU (formerly Art. 214(2) EC)), and the right of censure against the Commissioners, enabling it to dismiss the entire Commission under Article 234 TFEU (formerly Art. 201 EC).
- The Commission is obliged to answer Parliament's questions, and must produce a general report which is discussed by the Parliament (Art. 230 TFEU).
- The Council of Ministers is obliged to report three times a year to the Parliament on its recent activity.
- The President of the Council of Ministers reports to the Parliament at the beginning of the year.
- The European Parliament also runs the Committee on Petitions and appoints a European Ombudsman to investigate maladministration in any of the Institutions of the EU.

📖 **REVISION NOTE**

The European Parliament, Council of Ministers and European Commission also have the ability to challenge each other's activities through the Articles 263 and 265 procedure, as they have unlimited standing to bring an action for judicial review under this procedure (see Chapter 4 on judicial review).

The Member States also have unlimited standing under this procedure, and therefore can also scrutinise the Institutions in this way.

Role of the European Courts

The jurisdiction of the European Courts is split between the Court of Justice of the European Union (formerly the ECJ), which has existed since the signing of the European Coal and Steel Community (ECSC) Treaty in 1952, and the General Court (formerly the CFI), which was created by the Single European Act in 1986.

The two courts share the case-load of European cases – the General Court was originally created in order to assist with the growing case law of the CJEU. For example, these courts will deal with matters arising in particular areas (which are dealt with in other parts of this book) such as judicial review under Articles 263 and 265 TFEU (see Chapter 4), enforcement proceedings against Member States (Chapter 3) and will hear preliminary references from national courts under Article 267 TFEU (see Chapter 5). The two courts exist in a limited sense within a hierarchy, as appeals can go from the General Court to the CJEU on a point of law. It is the case that the more significant cases (in terms of importance) will go to the CJEU, and the less important cases will go to the General Court.

❗ Don't be tempted to . . .

Don't assume that the system of precedent you are used to in the English legal system will also apply in the EU. There is no system of binding precedent in the EU court system, unlike in the UK, where lower courts have to follow the rulings of higher ones. The CJEU, however, does operate a system of persuasive precedent, in that it is unlikely to depart from previous decisions in the interests of consistency but retains the freedom to do so if it feels it is appropriate.

■ The relationship between the Institutions

From the above concerning how the Institutions work, we must focus upon the information about how the Institutions relate to each other (Figure 2.3), and therefore how this can have an effect on the operation of the EU. This would also be important in approaching the essay

Figure 2.3

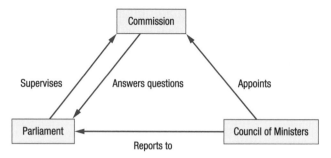

question at the beginning of this chapter. Below are some illustrations of those relationships.

Institutions	Relationship
Commission and Parliament	Parliament supervises Commission through power of censure and right to ask questions
Commission and Council of Ministers	Council submits policy to Commission to be legislated upon and delegates power to Commission through Comitology. Commission drafts legislation
Parliament and Council of Ministers	Parliament is consulted on legislative proposals. Council of Ministers reports to Parliament three times a year on activity

 Make your answer stand out

The relationship between the Institutions is rather complex, and certainly more so than can be represented here. However, in order to do well in assessment questions in this area, it is important to examine the subject in more detail. For example, see Lang (2006). This article examines the system of checks and balances referred to as the 'Community method', and argues that part of the criticism of the legal and political safeguards comes from this method being misunderstood.

If you can show that you have an understanding of the relationships between the Institutions, then this demonstrates that your knowledge of the operation of the EU goes beyond the merely factual regarding their composition and procedures.

Political influences between the Institutions

The Institutions all represent different interests within the EU, and therefore when considering their exercise of powers, it is important to remember who they represent. The European Commission, although appointed by the Member States, is intended to be an independent Institution, free from control of the Member State governments, and representative of the interests of the EU as a whole. This is also linked to the current thinking that there does not need to be a Commissioner from every Member State in each Commission. The Council of Ministers represents the interests of the Member State governments, and therefore its decision-making will be influenced by them, and the European Parliament is directly elected by the citizens of the EU, and will therefore take into account the interests of citizens. Bearing this in mind will therefore help with understanding the legislative and supervisory processes within the EU.

■ Putting it all together

Answer guidelines

See the essay question at the start of the chapter.

Approaching the question

This question asks about the 'Institutional balance' within the EU, and the quote refers to a system of checks and balances operating between these Institutions.

This is intended to allow you to analyse the relationship between the Institutions and the way in which they are able to monitor or supervise each other. You should bear in mind all the discussion about the powers of the Institutions, where they have the ability to monitor each other, and how problems may be dealt with. This is as much about the overall context and system that these Institutions operate in, and it is important not to get bogged down in just relaying a list of facts about each Institution in turn.

Significantly, the question includes a quote from 2002, and the question itself asks you to consider the extent to which the Institutional balance may have changed. This therefore requires you to consider the development of the EU through the Lisbon Treaty.

▶

Important points to include

To answer this question, you need to take into account the following:

- The basic make-up of the Institutions mentioned in the question, and who they represent.
- The powers of those Institutions, and how they are able to use them in a supervisory capacity, including:
    - ☐ The European Parliament's power of censure over the Commission.
    - ☐ The requirement for the Council and Commission to report to the Parliament.
    - ☐ The power of appointment of the Commission of the Council, and the power of approval of those appointments by the Parliament.
    - ☐ The standing of the Institutions to take action under judicial review against any of the other Institutions.
    - ☐ The effect of the recognition of the European Council as an EU Institution in the Lisbon Treaty.
    - ☐ An analysis of how this impacts upon the operation of the EU Institutions, especially with regard to how this may influence their decision-making.
- You should also take into account the effect that the new office of President of the European Council, along with the new Treaty recognition of the European Council, might have upon your answer to this question – has the balance shifted away from any of the other Institutions?

 Make your answer stand out

This question will require a certain amount of recall of information about the powers and duties of the Institutions, but, in order to make your answer rise above one which merely repeats this information, you need to think about how what you know about the Institutions allows you to analyse the relationship between them. Therefore, you need to think about how the elements of supervision between the Institutions might lead to an overall 'balance' between them, and how the power to make legislation is shared amongst them.

READ TO IMPRESS

Dashwood, A. and Johnson, A. (2004) 'The Institutions of the Enlarged EU under the Regime of the Constitutional Treaty', 41 CMLR 1481

Lang, J.T. (2006) 'Checks and Balances in the European Union: The Institutional Structure and the "Community Method"', 12 EPL 127

Peterson, J. and Bomberg, E. (1999) *Decision-Making in the European Union*. New York: Palgrave Macmillan

www.pearsoned.co.uk/lawexpress

 Go online to access more revision support including quizzes to test your knowledge, sample questions with answer guidelines, podcasts you can download, and more!

Articles 258–260 TFEU

Enforcement actions against Member States

Revision checklist

Essential points you should know:

☐ The purpose of enforcement actions against Member States, and their importance in ensuring the efficient functioning of the EU

☐ The substance and procedure of actions to be taken under Articles 258, 259 and 260

☐ The exercise of discretion by the Commission regarding Article 258

☐ Circumstances where Member States pursue an action under Article 259

■ Topic map

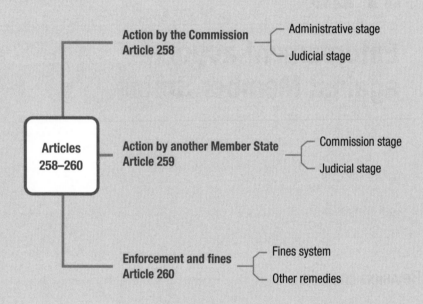

■ Introduction

An important part of the functioning of the EU is the enforceability of its laws.

Previously (in Chapter 2) we examined the Institutions' involvement in making law and (in Chapter 1) the EU's status in the legal systems of its Member States. However, at some point, whether it be deliberate or accidental, Member States run into problems of non-compatibility or conflict with EU law. We have seen a bit of the issue this creates (in Chapter 1) from the perspective of what happens at national level, but there are also consequences at EU level.

In such situations, there are mechanisms involving the European Commission and the Member States, which ensure that the conflict is resolved in the interests of the Single European Market and integration. There is a fairly straightforward procedure for dealing with infringements, and this chapter reviews the procedure for bringing enforcement proceedings and the principles that such an action must abide by, and discusses the reasons behind the procedure and its use. The procedure itself is fairly mechanistic, but the important thing to remember is the thinking behind having such a procedure in place.

ASSESSMENT ADVICE

Essay questions

This area is rather descriptive – there is a procedure for enforcing law against the Member States – and it has not tended to be an area which is as appropriate for essay questions as it is for problem questions. However, where there are essays, they may cover areas of the procedure such as, for example, the Commission's exercise of its discretion in using Article 258, or the effectiveness of the fines system in Article 260. These types of questions do not merely require you to regurgitate information in the exam, but rather require you to think critically about the procedure and its operation.

Problem questions

This area of law is one which can be combined with others in such a question, mainly because the problem itself could cover a substantive area of EU law, like free movement of goods or workers, but because of the nature of the problem (if it is caused by a Member State) then Articles 258–260 may help you to explain how it may be practically resolved. Therefore it would not be unusual for a question to have elements of this area as part of its solution, even though it does not appear to cover this topic.

■ Sample question

Could you answer this question? Below is a typical problem question that could arise on this topic. Guidelines on answering the question are included at the end of this chapter, whilst a sample essay question and guidance on tackling it can be found on the companion website.

PROBLEM QUESTION

The German government has recently introduced a system of import licences regarding the import of sausages into Germany. Any sausages with a fat content of more than 20 per cent are refused a licence under their scheme. The German Agriculture Minister, von Smallhausen, explains to the Council of Ministers that although this is regrettable, it is necessary in order to protect the wellbeing of the German people, and is part of a health policy committed to reducing the cholesterol levels of its citizens.

John Prestwick, the UK Minister of Agriculture, is incensed at this licensing scheme, and believes it is nothing more than a transparent ruse to maintain the market dominance of the German sausage producers and exclude the Great British Sausage from the German market during an economic downturn in meat products.

Prestwick writes a letter to von Smallhausen, stating that 'unless the German government drops this idiotic licence system, I shall ask the Commission to bring the German government, Parliament and Courts before the Court of Justice for blatantly conspiring to ignore Germany's obligations towards the Free Movement of Goods principle under the EC Treaty. Failing this, the UK government will take this matter before the Court itself.'

When the UK government raises this matter with the Commission, it replies that 'in the light of the current situation with the accession of new Member States into the EU and the effect of the transitional provisions involved in this, it may be better to leave this matter to next year, when the EU as a whole is more settled'.

Advise the UK government as to the possible legal remedies open to it under the TFEU.

■ Purpose of Articles 258–260 TFEU

The procedure in Articles 258–260 is there to ensure that where Member States are not complying with EU law, there is an effective system of ensuring that they do comply. This has three elements to it:

- Responsibility and powers as 'watchdog' given to a EU Institution.
- Power given to all Member States to take action where they see it is appropriate.
- System of fines to back up the system where necessary.

The way in which this system is put into practice is through a two-stage process:

- Action taken by, or in front of, the Commission.
- Cases taken to the CJEU either by the Commission or by another Member State.

□ REVISION NOTE

One other way in which Member States can be liable for their failure to enact EU laws in their own systems is through the doctrine of direct effect (discussed in Chapter 1). This is different from Articles 258–260 actions, because it can be pursued by individuals, and Articles 258–260 cannot. The emphasis is also different as direct effect is about giving effect to the law despite the actions of the Member State, and through the use of state liability for non-implementation, individuals can be compensated for damage which comes directly from the State's failure. Articles 258–260 are about pursuit and punishment of the Member State to ensure that it rectifies the problem, rather than compensation for individuals. They are two different ways in which action against Member States can be taken where they are not complying with EU law – the procedure is similar, but one action is taken by the Commission, the other by another Member State.

■ Article 258 TFEU: action by the Commission

KEY STATUTE

Article 258 TFEU

If the Commission considers that a Member State has failed to fulfil an obligation under this Treaty, it shall deliver a reasoned opinion on the matter after giving the State concerned the opportunity to submit its observations.

If the State concerned does not comply with the opinion within the period laid down by the Commission, the latter may bring the matter before the Court of Justice of the European Union.

Failure to fulfil an obligation

This is not defined in the Treaty. However, you should take a common-sense approach to looking at this issue – any duty or obligation placed on a Member State that it has not complied with can fall under this definition – whether that is an obligation directly from the

Treaty, or from some form of secondary legislation which has not been properly enacted under the Treaty. Also, it can either be an *action* or an *omission* by the Member State. You should also bear in mind that it doesn't matter which part of the State has failed to meet an obligation: the State as a whole is responsible – see Case 77/69 *Commission* v *Belgium* [1970] ECR 237, where the Belgian government was held to account for the failure of the Belgian Parliament to enact the relevant legislation. This can also apply to other parts of the State too, like the judiciary. There are parallels between this point and State Liability for Non-Implementation (see Chapter 1) because in that situation the State is liable regardless of which state organ is responsible.

Member State obligations and the Treaty

All Member States have a general obligation to observe and not contradict EU law. This used to be contained in Article 10 of the Treaty of Rome, but post-Lisbon this has now been moved to Article 4(3) of the TEU.

KEY STATUTE

Article 4(3) TEU

The Member States shall take any appropriate measure, general or particular, to ensure fulfilment of the obligations arising out of the Treaties or resulting from acts of the Institutions of the Union.

✎ EXAM TIP

This Article is always worth bearing in mind whenever considering any obligation owed by the Member States, not just those under Articles 258–260, and it binds all organs of the state concerned, including government departments, state-funded agencies, local government, etc. It is one of those very general pieces of EU law that underpins EU membership generally and is therefore very useful to know.

Procedure under Article 258 TFEU

As mentioned above, there are two elements to this after informal discussions have taken place between the Member State and the Commission – action by the Commission, and action in the CJEU. The procedure is shown in Figure 3.1.

Figure 3.1

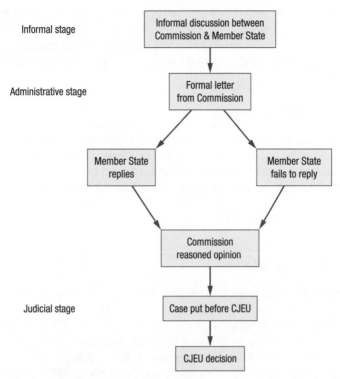

Procedure	What it means
Informal letter	The Commission communicates informally and in private with a Member State about a potential breach under the Treaty. The Member State has to cooperate under its obligations in Article 4(3) TEU
Formal notice	Formal written letter from the Commission to the Member State. Sets out what they are accused of, and asks them to respond
Member State response	Written response to formal notice. If the Member State fails to respond in two months, the Commission goes on to the next stage anyway
Commission's reasoned opinion	Formal opinion from the Commission stating what the infringement is, and requiring the Member State to fix the problem. Includes a time limit for them to do so (usually two months)

Administrative stage

This procedure must be followed by the Commission, otherwise the Member State has cause to complain about its use of the procedure under Article 263 or 265 TFEU. However, if this procedure is properly followed and the Member State does not comply with the Commission's **reasoned opinion**, then the Commission may move on to the next stage of the procedure.

KEY DEFINITION: Reasoned opinion

The reasoned opinion is a written statement from the Commission, which lays down the obligation concerned, and the reasons why the Commission believes the Member State has failed to meet this obligation. It should clearly spell out the Commission's objection, and therefore it should be clear to the Member State what it needs to do to rectify the problem.

! Don't be tempted to . . .

Don't assume that because the Commission has a power to take action, that it can be compelled to do so. The important point to make here is the discretion that the Commission has in bringing this procedure. Article 258 says '*If* the Commission considers that a Member State has failed to fulfil an obligation . . .' The Commission has a lot of discretion as to when it is going to take action, and for which infringements. Case 247/87 *Star Fruit Company* v *Commission* [1989] ECR 291 shows that the Commission can't be forced to take action under Article 258.

There is also no time limit on the different actions of the Commission under the administrative stage, and so it can take the next step in the process when it wishes, if at all. About 90 per cent of all Article 258 actions are resolved in this stage without going to the CJEU, and the way in which the Commission manages these situations is part of this.

You should bear in mind that as a result an individual cannot force the Commission to take action, but a Member State can take action itself under Article 259. An individual is better off trying to use direct effect to apply the law in question in the Member State, as this allows them to seek a remedy in a national court, and this can be somewhat speedier. Any problems requiring the interpretation of the CJEU can then be referred under the Article 267 procedure.

When revising this subject, remember that there are alternatives, and that this procedure is part of a wider system. This can be an important point to remember in a problem question such as the one at the beginning of this chapter, but also in an essay question about the Commission's discretion in Article 258.

Make your answer stand out

Commission discretion is an important part of the flexibility of the Article 258 procedure – the Commission makes its own decisions as to which actions to pursue, but at the same time it means it can go after the more serious infringements first. This flexibility is an important part of making sure that the procedure is effectively applied. For further reading on this, see Evans (1979). See also Case 7/71 *Commission* v *France* for further guidance from AG Roemer on when the Commission might be justified in exercising its discretion not to take action.

Judicial stage

Once the Commission has exhausted the administrative stage, if the Member State does not comply with its reasoned opinion within the time limit, then the Commission may take the matter to the CJEU. This is the judicial stage.

Points to bear in mind concerning the judicial stage:

■ The burden of proof lies with the Commission to prove its case.

■ Even if the Member State has complied with the reasoned opinion by the time the case comes to court, the Commission may still bring the case: see Case C-240/86 *Commission* v *Greece* [1988] ECR 1835 which confirmed that Member States are obliged to comply with the Commission.

■ Defences put forward by the Member States are generally not accepted by the CJEU (see, for example, Case 128/78 *Re: Tachographs* (*Commission* v *UK*) [1979] ECR 419 – political difficulties involving disputes with the transport unions were not an acceptable reason not to introduce new tachograph laws in the UK). The only acceptable defence is that the Commission got it wrong, and that the State is not in breach of EU law. See also Case 77/69 *Commission* v *Belgium* and Case C-56/90 *Commission* v *UK* for other examples.

The outcome of a case in the CJEU is as described in Article 260, as follows.

KEY STATUTE

Article 260(1) TFEU

If the Court of Justice finds that a Member State has failed to fulfil an obligation under this Treaty, the State shall be required to take the necessary measures to comply with the judgment of the Court of Justice.

The key thing to remember here is that this therefore provides a clear obligation for the Member State to follow, and removes any ambiguity that the action itself might have uncovered. The Member State *has* to comply – and if they fail to do so, this is where Article 260(2) comes in (this is dealt with later in this chapter).

■ Article 259 TFEU: action by another Member State

Although the Commission cannot be forced to take action, another Member State has the ability to take the matter to the CJEU itself, if the Commission fails to do so. This takes place under Article 259. A Member State may choose to take this action if it feels the matter is important enough for it to be urgently addressed under the Article 258–260 procedure.

KEY STATUTE

Article 259(1) TFEU

A Member State which considers that another Member State has failed to fulfil an obligation under this Treaty may bring the matter before the Court of Justice.

Procedure under Article 259

The procedure (Figure 3.2) followed here is very similar to that of Article 258. Article 259(2) states that the matter has to be brought before the Commission by the Member State that is raising the complaint before it can go to the CJEU, so the Commission still has an

Figure 3.2

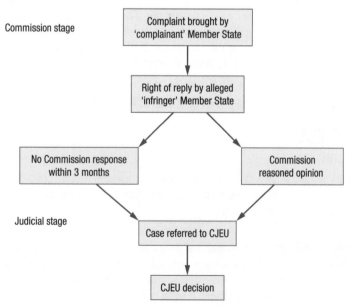

involvement here. However, the Commission's role is reduced to hearing both States' submissions on the matter and then putting forward a reasoned opinion.

✎ **EXAM TIP**

Although the Commission is still involved in Article 259, remember that it is not able to delay or dictate the timing of the action taken here. This may be important if the Commission refused to take action itself under Article 258. It is also important to remember this if you are being asked to advise a Member State in a problem question.

There is a time limit of three months, and if within that time the Commission has not issued a reasoned opinion, then the Member State is able to take its case to the CJEU without one.

Problems with Article 259 TFEU

There are several reasons why Article 259 actions can be problematic. Member States are reluctant to take action because of the ensuing diplomatic fallout. It can be a device for forcing the Commission to take the matter further, as shown in Case C-1/00 *Commission* v *France* where the UK initially said it was going to take action against France for its refusal to lift the beef ban after the BSE crisis. The Commission eventually took action itself.

Article 259 actions that go all the way to the CJEU are rare. This is mainly because it is much more straightforward to get the Commission to pursue the action under Article 258 (as seen in the *Commission* v *France* case above). There have been only three cases to date that resulted in a judgment from the CJEU: Case 141/78 *France* v *UK* [1979] ECR 2923, Case C-388/95 *Belgium* v *Spain* [2000] ECR I-3123 and Case C-145/04 *Spain* v *UK* [2006] ECR I-7917.

■ Article 260 TFEU: enforcement and fines

Usually, a successful action under Article 258 or 259 will result in the Member State complying with its obligations under the Treaty. The declaration by the CJEU that the Member State is acting incompatibly with EU law is usually enough confirmation to the Member State that it needs to change its actions, and so therefore it complies. In a few very unusual situations it may be necessary to use the enforcement section of Article 260. This requires a second action in the CJEU in order to decide on the fine amount to be imposed upon the Member State.

Factors that are taken into account when deciding the amount to fine are:

- the seriousness of the breach and the length of time that has passed since that breach;
- the financial size (by gross domestic product) of the Member State;
- whether to impose a lump sum fine, or one which increases daily.

 Make your answer stand out

Article 260's fines system was only introduced in order to give more teeth to enforcement of EU law against the Member States in more recent times – without it, a State could ignore political pressure from the EU and continue to act in infringement of its obligations. This system aims to avoid cases lingering for many years. If you are dealing with an essay question on the effectiveness of the enforcement proceedings under Articles 258–260, then a discussion of the development and effectiveness of the fines system will show a deeper appreciation of the evolution of this procedure. See Wenneras (2006).

Also, when discussing the fines system, it is important to show an understanding of the factors that contribute to the size and type of penalty applied – see the bullet points just before this box.

Penalties for failing to implement a Directive: the new regime

Ordinarily the Commission would need to go through two actions in order to impose penalties upon an infringing State (the original Article 258 action and an Article 260 action) that is failing to comply with EU law, but now Article 260(3) has added some teeth to the Article 258 procedure by allowing for penalties to be applied on the first occasion that the matter goes to the CJEU. Please bear in mind that this only applies to a failure to implement a Directive.

KEY STATUTE

Article 260(3) TFEU

When the Commission brings a case before the Court pursuant to Article 258 on the grounds that the Member State concerned has failed to fulfil its obligation to notify measures transposing a directive adopted under a legislative procedure, it may, when it deems appropriate, specify the amount of the lump sum or penalty payment to be paid by the Member State concerned which it considers appropriate in the circumstances.

If the Court finds that there is an infringement it may impose a lump sum or penalty payment on the Member State concerned not exceeding the amount specified by the Commission. The payment obligation shall take effect on the date set by the Court in its judgment.

Therefore, if an action is about *failure to implement a Directive*, the Commission may apply for a penalty to be levied against the infringing Member State in the first case, and not have to take the procedure around for a second time.

 Make your answer stand out

- This new provision is all about tightening up the procedures under Article 258. Delays in the procedure are an important consideration, and this prevents Member States taking advantage of the fact that lengthy enforcement procedures will allow them more time before they are forced to implement new Directives.

- This also highlights the importance of Directives to the legal regime at EU level. This added part of Article 260 only applies to Directives, and shows how serious a failure to implement a Directive is in the EU legal system.

- If you are faced with a problem question in an assessment involving failure to implement, then this could allow you to show a deeper understanding of how the fines system works, and how it has been updated to deal with States who flagrantly breach EU law.

- If you are faced with an essay question on this area, it can allow you to show an understanding of the way in which the procedure has developed.

Other remedies available in Articles 258–260 actions

Articles 258–260 actions can be very lengthy. Some cases can drag on for years, the most extreme example being the *Commission* v *France* case (Case C-177/04 [2006] ECR I-2461) which lasted from 1973 to 1994! It may be necessary to make interim orders – those that provide a temporary solution to the problem while the case is still being decided.

Treaty Article	Description
Article 278	Interim injunction from CJEU to suspend a piece of legislation from a Member State that is breaching EU law
Article 279	Interim measures which can be put in place by the CJEU where there is damage to an individual's interests or economic hardship

■ Putting it all together

Answer guidelines

See the problem question at the start of the chapter.

Approaching the question

This question requires a knowledge of two areas: Articles 258–260 as covered in this chapter, but also free movement of goods (as discussed in Chapter 7). The basic points on free movement of goods will be mentioned here, but you will need to look at the relevant law in that chapter. Remember that this question is asking you to analyse the situation from the point of view of the UK government. Your answer will need to discuss the relevant law with a view to advising the UK government on what it can do as a result of this problem. This therefore means that there are two elements to this question: a *procedural* element and a *substantive* element. The information and knowledge from this chapter deals with the *procedural* part of your answer to the question – how the Articles 258–260 procedure can help the government resolve the problem it has.

Important points to include

You will need to bear in mind the following issues in your answer:

- The most likely breach of Germany's obligations is through the free movement of goods provisions in Article 34.

- The licensing restrictions are likely to be seen as a measure having an equivalent effect to a quantitative restriction (**MEQR**).

- The attempt to justify the breach by claiming that the German government is protecting the health of the German people is likely to be dismissed following the *Cassis de Dijon* case (see Chapter 6 for details of this).

- So, you need to look at Article 258, if it is to be invoked, how it would be used here, and whether the Commission can be forced to act here. Discuss the Commission's discretion, and its reasons behind not acting – are these appropriate? See the section on the Commission's discretion earlier in this chapter.

- What procedure would need to be followed? Break it down into administrative and judicial procedure and explain what is needed in each one, along with things like time limits – these can help you to discuss the possible delays in using this procedure.

■ If the Commission is unwilling to follow the Article 258 procedure, look at Article 259 as an alternative – what right does the UK government have to bring the action? Examine the way in which it would do this, what the procedure involves, and, as this would be invoked as a result of the Commission's refusal to take action, consider the influence of the Commission on how quickly an Article 259 action can proceed (there are time limits that allow a Member State to continue the procedure if the Commission fails to respond).

■ Finally, Article 260(2) should be used if the German government still refuses to cooperate, as this can impose a fine upon it for non-compliance. Make sure you discuss the factors that influence how large, and of what type, the fine is likely to be – this will have a bearing upon the way in which the German government is likely to react to a successful action against it. Remember, Article 260(3) doesn't apply here, as this is not about a Directive – however, if you encounter an exam question involving a Directive, you will need to look into this as well.

 Make your answer stand out

As this is an area heavily dominated by procedure, it is easy just to list the procedure as your answer. However, this will result in an answer that is heavily descriptive and unlikely to impress your examiner. Take some time to think about the policy behind the procedure. The Commission's discretion allows flexibility in the application of Article 258, for example. Similarly, Article 259 is used rarely because of the potential for political problems. Also, the factors involved in determining fines, and reasons for Commission inaction in certain situations will all require you to analyse the facts of the scenario. Examiners like students to have analysed a situation and to be able to produce answers which demonstrate a good understanding of the area, rather than ones that show they have just memorised a lot of facts and reproduced them. Merely repeating the procedure in the hope that the examiner will draw the connection between the procedure and the situation is poor technique and does not demonstrate that you have a full understanding of this area.

READ TO IMPRESS

Evans, A. (1979) 'The Enforcement Procedure of Article 169 EEC: Commission Discretion', 4 EL Rev 442 (Art. 169 is the old numbering for Art. 258)

Wenneras, P. (2006) 'A New Dawn for Commission Enforcement under Articles 226 and 228 EC: General and Persistent (GAP) Infringements, Lump Sums and Penalty Payments', 43 CML Rev 31 (Arts. 226 and 228 are now Arts. 258 and 260)

www.pearsoned.co.uk/lawexpress

Go online to access more revision support including quizzes to test your knowledge, sample questions with answer guidelines, podcasts you can download, and more!

Articles 263 & 265 TFEU

Judicial review

4

Revision checklist

Essential points you should know:

☐ The underlying purpose for judicial review actions in the CJEU

☐ The EU Acts that can be annulled and the grounds for that annulment

☐ The Institutions that can be compelled to act in the absence of action, and the grounds for this

☐ The *locus standi* of an applicant for an action under Articles 263 or 265

☐ The unity principle binding Articles 263 and 265 together

■ Topic map

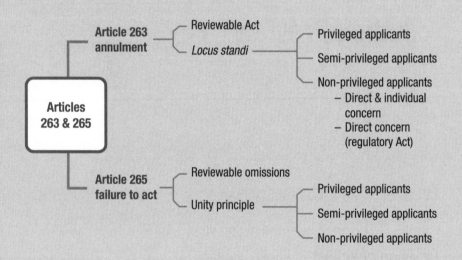

■ Introduction

The ability to challenge a binding Act of the EU, or a failure by an Institution to act, through judicial review is an important part of the EU's legal system.

Articles 263 and 265 contain the main procedures for judicial review of EU law. Although there is no official constitution of the EU, the TEU and the TFEU both confer powers and obligations upon the EU Institutions, and therefore there needs to be a mechanism whereby the exercise (or not) of powers can be reviewed, and the Institutions properly held to account. These procedures have two purposes, either to annul an improperly enacted law, or to compel an institution of the EU to act in a situation where it has not done so, in contravention of its duties under the Treaties.

This procedure is important because of the way that it fits in with the system of checks and balances within the EU – it allows the Institutions, the Member States and individuals to scrutinise EU law and therefore ensure that powers are not being abused.

The purpose of this chapter is to examine these two treaty Articles and the circumstances in which they may come into play. This covers:

■ the types of Act that may be challenged, and

■ the types of failure to act that may be challenged,

as well as the grounds upon which they may be challenged. The other important issue concerns the rules governing who can challenge, which are stricter for individuals wishing to challenge an **EU Act**, rather than for a Member State or an Institution. This last issue will be dealt with separately.

ASSESSMENT ADVICE

Essay questions

Essay questions in this area tend to focus upon some aspect of the judicial review mechanism. This can be, for example, the role this procedure has to play in the checks and balances system set up between the Institutions; it can also be the difficulty which an individual faces in establishing *locus standi* and a discussion of the case law surrounding this issue. Often they concern the development of the judicial review system, or the effect of that system on the institutional balance within the EU. ▶

Problem questions

Problem questions, on the other hand, are more unusual, as they have to involve the creation of a scenario. This therefore can tend to focus upon the *locus standi* issue, as this will involve individuals, and allows students to focus upon the effect that the rules have upon the decision-making process at EU level.

Sample question

Could you answer this question? Below is a typical essay question that could arise on this topic. Guidelines on answering the question are included at the end of this chapter, whilst a sample problem question and guidance on tackling it can be found on the companion website.

ESSAY QUESTION

EU law 'positively discriminates' against any natural or legal person who might wish to pursue an action under Articles 263 and 265.

Discuss the above statement, in particular the way in which the changes brought in by the Lisbon Treaty might have affected this statement.

Article 263 TFEU: annulment of an Act of the EU

KEY STATUTE

Article 263(1) TFEU

The Court of Justice shall review the legality of Acts adopted jointly by the European Parliament and the Council, of Acts of the Council, of the Commission and of the European Central Bank, other than recommendations and opinions, and of Acts of the European Parliament intended to produce legal effects *vis-à-vis* third parties. It shall also review the legality of Acts of bodies, offices or agencies of the Union intended to produce legal effects *vis-à-vis* third parties.

Article 263 is the EU's judicial review procedure (Figure 4.1) – allowing the Court of Justice of the European Union to review binding Acts of the EU. The purpose of the procedure is to

Figure 4.1

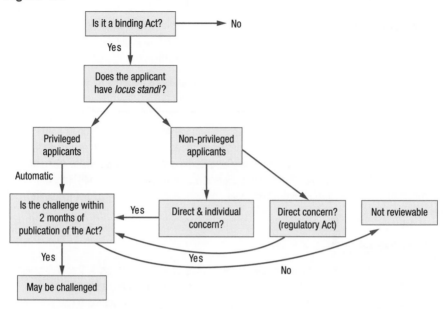

ensure accountability of the Institutions for action taken by them, and to allow different parties to challenge them.

■ Reviewable Acts

Article 263 states that any Act of the EU, other than recommendations and opinions, can be reviewed. With the introduction of the Lisbon Treaty, the law has been changed to accommodate *other Acts of the EU that produce legal effects*. Previously it was restricted only to those Acts found in Article 288 (formerly 249), however the law has now changed to accommodate the already established reasoning of the CJEU (formerly ECJ) on this matter. The key issue here lies with the binding nature of the Act – recommendations and opinions are not reviewable because they are not binding, and therefore annulling them will have no effect. However, any other Act of the EU which produces legal effects can be challenged. For example, all of the following have been held to be subject to review under the then Article 230 (now 263):

Name of case	Type of EU Act
Case 294/83 *Parti Ecologiste (Les Verts)* v *European Parliament*	Measures adopted by the European Parliament intended to have legal effects *vis-à-vis* third parties ▶

Name of case	Type of EU Act
Case 22/70 *Commission* v *Council*	A resolution adopted by the Council of Ministers to participate in the European Road Transport Agreement
Cases 193 & 194/87 *Maurissen and Others* v *Court of Auditors*	A measure adopted by the Court of Auditors

The key point here is that the Act itself causes a change to the legal position of some person or organisation within the EU. Any Act which does this can be challenged under the judicial review procedure. For example, Case 60/81 *International Business Machines* v *Commission* [1981] ECR 2639 involved a situation where a letter sent to IBM by the Commission did nothing to change their legal position, and therefore was not judicially reviewable.

📖 **REVISION NOTE**

Only secondary sources of law are dealt with by this area of the Treaty – Treaty Articles themselves cannot be challenged. (See Chapter 1 for a fuller examination of those sources of law.) In this chapter, where it refers to an 'EU Act', it concerns these secondary sources of law.

■ *Locus standi*: the ability to challenge an Act

Probably the most important aspect of Article 263 is the ability to challenge an Act. If you do not have *locus standi*, then you cannot take action here. Lack of *locus standi* will result in a case being thrown out immediately. This is also important for the ability to challenge failure to act in Article 265. Because the rules are applied similarly in both Articles, we can examine the *locus standi* rules for both Treaty Articles together.

For the purposes of Articles 263 and 265, those eligible to challenge a EU Act (or failure to act) are split into three categories:

Category	Members of this category
Privileged applicants	Commission, Council of Ministers, European Parliament, all Member States
Semi-privileged applicants	European Central Bank, Court of Auditors, Committee of the Regions
Non-privileged applicants	Private individuals (including companies)

Privileged applicants

KEY STATUTE

Article 263(2) TFEU

[The CJEU] shall for this purpose have jurisdiction in actions brought by a Member State, the European Parliament, the Council or the Commission on grounds of lack of competence, infringement of an essential procedural requirement, infringement of this Treaty or of any rule of law relating to its application, or misuse of powers.

Those in this category are deemed to have a general interest in EU Acts, and therefore can challenge any reviewable Act. The fact that these parties will all have taken part in some way in passing this legislation in the first place does not disqualify them. This point was made in Case 166/78 *Italy* v *EC Council* [1979] ECR 2575. The European Parliament has only been added to this category in the recent past, as part of the increase in its influence and power within the EU.

✎ EXAM TIP

The exercise of Articles 263 and 265 is an important part of the system of 'checks and balances' within the EU. In particular, because the European Parliament now has privileged applicant status, it adds to its supervisory powers. Any answer to an essay question concerning the supervisory powers of the European Parliament (see Chapter 2) should discuss this issue, and any answer to a question set by your examiners which asks you to comment on the developing powers of the European Parliament should make this point.

Semi-privileged applicants

KEY STATUTE

Article 263(3) TFEU

The Court of Justice shall have jurisdiction under the same conditions in actions brought by the Court of Auditors, by the European Central Bank and by the Committee of the Regions for the purpose of protecting their prerogatives.

The Court of Auditors and the European Central Bank have always been able to challenge an EU Act if the law in question affects or changes one of their powers. Now the Committee of the Regions is also able to exercise this power.

Non-privileged applicants

KEY STATUTE

Article 263(4) TFEU

Any natural or legal person may, under the conditions laid down in the first and second paragraphs, institute proceedings against an Act addressed to that person or which is of direct and individual concern to them, and against a regulatory Act which is of direct concern to them and does not entail implementing measures.

Private persons and companies are classed as 'non-privileged' because they have to prove that they should be entitled to challenge an EU Act. This is the most controversial area of this subject because, first, it is in direct contrast to the position of privileged applicants, and, secondly, it very heavily restricts a non-privileged applicant's ability to challenge an Act. The wording of Article 263(4) has changed slightly from that of the former Article 230(4). Article 263(4) allows an individual to challenge an Act where:

- it concerns an Act addressed to the person;

- it concerns an Act addressed to another person which is of *direct and individual* concern to the applicant; or

- it concerns a regulatory Act, which is of *direct concern* to the applicant, and which does not entail implementing measures.

The previous system under former Article 230 was very strict, and heavily restricted the type of EU Act which could be challenged. The new post-Lisbon system is broader, mainly because of the use of 'Act' instead of 'decision' in the wording of Article 263 – this opens up possibilities of a wide range of EU Acts being challengeable, but also because of the 'regulatory Act' provision – this does not have the same requirement of 'individual concern' – but still restricts the circumstances in which an Act can be challenged.

The first of the three categories above will be fairly easy to deal with – Acts addressed to individuals are self-evident. If the Act is addressed to you, then you are assumed to be able to challenge it due to the fact that it is going to have a real legal effect upon you; whether you are an individual or a company or other organisation within the EU. Therefore the position for individuals in this type of situation is that they must show that it is an Act of the EU that they are raising an issue about, and that Act is of direct and individual concern to the person.

The right to challenge an 'Act'

To see how the new system has liberalised judicial review by individuals, it is necessary to examine the old system. This restricted individuals to challenge only those Acts equivalent to a decision. For example, in Case 41–44/70 *International Fruit Co.* v *Commission* [1971] ECR 411, it was held that if a Regulation could be regarded as equivalent to a decision (and therefore was applied like one), then it could be challenged, but ordinarily Regulations have general application, and so cannot be challenged by an individual. This is because it is very difficult to establish individual concern in a situation where the regulation applies to everyone equally. Therefore, the CJEU would have to be convinced that the Regulation was merely a 'disguised decision' in order for that person to show they were 'individually concerned'.

The table on page 69 gives some indication of the European Courts' relaxing of attitudes – the case below gives further indication of this.

Make your answer stand out

Case C-309/89 *Codorniu* v *EC Council* [1994] ECR I-1853 relaxed the rules on whether Regulations with general application could be challenged by individuals. Although normally any Act of general application cannot be challenged by individuals, in *Codorniu* the Regulation did have general application, but could still be challenged because it had particular concern to Codorniu. This was a bold move because the Court of Justice was saying that it had both general and specific applications at the same time. Unfortunately this has not had the effect of generally relaxing the rules, as it hasn't subsequently been followed. The changes to the Treaty in this area do look like they have followed some of the principles from *Codorniu* though. A discussion of the development of this area is essential in an essay that asks you to discuss the impact of the *Codorniu* case.

See Arnull (2001).

An Act addressed to that person

Where an Act is addressed to a particular person, then they will have *locus standi* to challenge it. With regard to the definition of 'Act', the *Codorniu* case, and the subsequent amendment brought in by the Lisbon Treaty has led to a more liberal system, whereby the category regarding what is challengeable has broadened out. The concept of 'Act' is much wider than that of 'decision', and there are now more opportunities for individuals to challenge the actions of the EU.

An Act of direct and individual concern to the person

Aside from an Act addressed to that person, if an Act is of direct and individual concern to that applicant, then they can also challenge. Again, the post-Lisbon concept of 'Act' is broader than previously, but we can use the earlier case law from the old Article 230 actions to define this concept.

Individual concern

The definition of individual concern does not come from the Treaties. It can be found in the following case.

KEY CASE

Case 25/62 Plaumann v Commission **[1963] ECR 95**

Concerning: the test for individual concern

Facts

This was a decision aimed at the German government instructing them to lift an import duty on clementines going into Germany. Plaumann claimed direct and individual concern with the decision addressed to the German government.

Legal principle

They would be individually concerned if the decision affected them 'by reason of certain attributes which are peculiar to them or by reason of circumstances in which they are differentiated from all other persons'.

This has therefore been described as defining someone as being part of a 'fixed, closed class'. The main problem that many applicants have had is in defining themselves in this way. There have been various failed attempts by applicants in defining themselves as part of this class. In the *Plaumann* case itself, Plaumann was unable to do so because its status of an importer of clementines did not make it different to all other persons – anyone, in theory, could import clementines. Most other failed attempts at establishing *locus standi* have also been importers, as in Case 11/82 *Piraiki-Patraiki* v *Commission*, or Case T-47/95 *Terres Rouges Consultant* v *EC Commission*, or the *Plaumann* case itself. The argument here was that although these persons defined themselves as importers, anyone could carry out that activity, and therefore they were not part of a fixed, closed class.

! Don't be tempted to . . .

The case law in this area has defined the concept of a fixed, closed class rather strictly. Following on from the test (above) in *Plaumann*, there have been several cases that denied *locus standi* to applicants on this basis. This is an important issue in answering questions on individual concern. For example, following the *Plaumann* criteria, in Case T-47/95 *Terres Rouges Consultant* v *EC Commission*, the court did not grant standing to a company that had a 70 per cent monopoly in importing bananas – because the class it was in could be joined by anyone else. The key here is: are you in a class that makes you different from everyone else, a class that cannot be joined by anyone else and a class which you cannot leave? If so, then you are in a fixed, closed class. Don't fall into the same trap that many of the importers in these cases did, by believing that just because they categorised themselves in a particular way, it would satisfy the test for individual concern. It *must* be a *fixed, closed* class. No one can join, and no one can leave this class.

If you look at the following case, you can see how an applicant can be shown to be part of a fixed, closed class.

KEY CASE

Cases 106 & 107/63 *Alfred Toepfer and Getreide-Import Gesellschaft* v *Commission* [1965] ECR 405

Concerning: the concept of 'fixed, closed class' for an importer

Facts

The applicants had applied for a licence to import grain into Germany on 1 October. The duty on this import was zero, but the German government had asked the Commission for permission to increase the duty. The Commission agreed, and added that in order to do this, all applications made on 1 October would be rejected, and the duty would be imposed from 2 October. The applicants challenged this decision.

Legal principle

The Court of Justice decided that they had standing because they were not just an importer as in the other cases listed above, but because they were part of a fixed closed class – those who had applied for an import licence on 1 October. This went beyond merely being importers as in *Plaumann*, but meant that they were part of a group who were individually affected by the decision. They were also a group that could be very specifically defined, and a group that it would be impossible for anyone else to join.

Aside from the *Codorniu* case above, the European Courts have shown a willingness to be more flexible with this concept. Some examples of the application of this are set out in the table below.

Individual concern	Case
As part of a class of political parties affected by the decision	Case 294/83 *'Les Verts'* v *Parliament* [1986] ECR 1339
If the applicant has been involved in the legislative process used to make the law	Case T-585/93 *Stichtig Greenpeace* v *Commission* [1995] ECR II-2205
If the applicant is a trade association representing the interests of those who are individually concerned	Cases T-447–449/93 *AITEC* v *Commission* [1995] ECR II-1971

Direct concern

Direct concern merely means that the EU Act is directly applicable to the individual, without any need for the Member States to enact any further laws or have any further discretion.

For example, in Cases 10 & 18/68 *Eridana* v *Commission* [1969] ECR 459, although this concerned granting of aid by the Commission, the decision as to who was given the aid was made by the Italian government. In this case, the measure was not of direct concern to the applicant as there was a further layer between the measure and the applicant.

✎ EXAM TIP

The consequence of such strict requirements for non-privileged applicants is that very few actions may be brought by private individuals. This may seem to be rather harsh; however, when discussing this area, it is worth remembering that there are also important policy reasons for doing this. If the *locus standi* test were broader, then the consequence would likely be the clogging of the European Courts with actions brought by those who aren't immediately affected by them. There are also other avenues for individuals to follow if they do not have *locus standi*, such as use of the principle of direct effects in national courts, and challenges to laws through the Article 267 reference procedure. You should bear all of this in mind, especially if your exam asks you to discuss the position of private parties under this action.

You should also be clear on the potential application of Article 263 now that it refers to 'Act' rather than 'decision', and is therefore likely to be wider in application than previously. This has effectively broadened the potential use of this procedure by ALL applicants, not just non-privileged ones.

A regulatory Act of direct concern which does not entail implementing measures

This is something new to the Treaty post-Lisbon, and therefore the meaning of 'regulatory Act' has not been completely clear. A common interpretation of this is to think of the type of 'decisions in the form of Regulations' that were mentioned in the *International Fruit* case above as falling into this category. However, the meaning of 'regulatory Act which does not require implementing measures' is not as straightforward as this, as is shown in the following cases.

KEY CASE

Case T-18/10 *Inuit Tapiriit Kanatami* v *European Parliament* [2012] All ER (EC) 183

Concerning: the meaning of 'regulatory Act' under Article 263(4)

Facts

This case concerned an EU Regulation regarding the import and sale of seal products in the EU. The case was brought by a group of seal hunters, trappers and those involved in processing seal products who sought to have the EU Regulation annulled. They claimed

---

that the Regulation was a 'regulatory Act' and therefore that they only needed to establish direct concern.

Legal principle

The General Court decided that the proper definition of 'regulatory Act' is that of a *non-legislative* Act that has *general* application, and the regulation in question did not satisfy this test due to its legislative nature. The claimants were therefore not granted *locus standi* due to the fact that, as a result, they would need to satisfy the general standing test, which included individual concern – they were unable to do so.

This led to the first case where the test of 'regulatory Act' was satisfied.

KEY CASE

Case T-262/10 *Microban International Ltd* v *European Commission* **[2012] All ER (EC) 595**

Concerning: the definition of 'regulatory Act' under Article 263(4)

Facts

This case concerned an American company which objected to a Commission Decision that triclosan could no longer be used in manufacture of plastics which could come into contact with food. The test discussed in *Inuit* (above) was used, that a 'regulatory Act' was a non-legislative one which had general application.

Legal principle

The General Court held that the Commission Decision satisfied the test, as it was non-legislative in nature, and also was of general application (it applied to everyone, not just the company that brought the case). As it was a ban, it also did not require implementing measures. The company bringing the case was able to show direct concern, and therefore was granted *locus standi.*

The consequence of this is that someone able to show that the Act in question is a regulatory Act which does not require further implementation will only have to show *direct concern* and not *individual concern* as with other 'Acts'. Although a little more restrictive than was originally thought, it still gives applicants for judicial review wider scope for challenge than exists in national legal systems.

Time limit

Article 263(5) sets a time limit of two months from date of publication, or from the date the applicant knew about the Act.

Reasons to challenge an EU act

Reason	Example
Lack of competence	Each Institution must only act within the powers given to it by the Treaty
	See Case C-327/91 *France* v *Commission* [1994] ECR I-3641 where the Commission signed an international agreement that should have been done by the Council
Infringement of an essential procedural requirement	Failing to follow proper procedure
	See Case 139/79 *Maizena* v *Council* [1980] ECR 3393 where the Council failed to consult the European Parliament, where they were obliged to under the Treaty
Infringement of the Treaty	A very broad term, which could include all general principles of EU law
	Case 101/76 *KSH* v *Intervention Board* [1977] ECR 797 involved the general principle of the right to be heard
Misuse of powers	Where an Institution uses its powers for the wrong purpose

■ Article 265 TFEU: action for failure to act

Actions under Articles 263 and 265 are very closely linked under the **unity principle**, therefore the rules concerning how these Articles are used run parallel. They can also be pleaded at the same time, because a failure to act can also be seen as an Institution acting improperly.

Locus standi

The rules concerning *locus standi* are similar but more restrictive than those for Article 263.

Article	Applicants
Article 265(1) – privileged applicants	Institutions as discussed in Article 263(2)
Article 265(3) – non-privileged applicants	Private individuals as discussed in Article 263(4)

! Don't be tempted to . . .

Don't think you can simply analogise Article 265 with 263. The main problem here is that Article 265 is even more restrictive than Article 263, *because it doesn't even allow applicants who have 'direct and individual concern'* as Article 263 does. The only individuals who can use Article 265 are those to whom a decision *should* have been addressed.

KEY CASE

Case 246/81 *Lord Bethel* v *Commission* [1982] ECR 2277

Concerning: locus standi *for an individual challenging a failure to act*

Facts

Lord Bethel challenged the Commission's failure to take action against airline price-fixing. The Commission claimed he did not have *locus standi*.

Legal principle

The ECJ (now CJEU) decided that as any decision from the Commission concerning the price-fixing would not be addressed to him, then he did not have standing to challenge the Commission's failure to act.

Reviewable omissions

Article 265 is about duties under the Treaty. So if an Institution has failed to act, and the Treaty states that they should have, then this may be a reviewable omission. It must be a clear duty under the Treaty, and so if this is not the case, then there is no action. For example, in Case 13/83 *European Parliament* v *Commission* [1985] ECR 1513, the obligation placed on the Commission by the Treaty was not worded precisely enough for a failure to perform this obligation to be a failure to act under the meaning of Article 265.

Article 265 procedure

! Don't be tempted to . . .

Where an Institution defines its position, this can be an easy way for it to avoid action under Article 265. The Treaty doesn't define what this is, but if an Institution justifies why it has not acted, then it may escape the action being brought under Article 265. The Court of Justice has held actions inadmissible where this was the case. This is therefore an easy way for an Institution to avoid having to act, and therefore will bring an end to the action. Please bear this in mind when answering an Article 265 question. The procedure under Article 265 is illustrated in Figure 4.2.

Figure 4.2

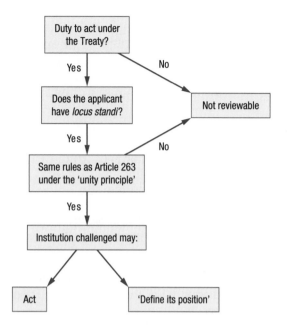

✎ **EXAM TIP**

Because the two areas of Articles 263 and 265 are so closely linked under the unity principle, it is worth thinking about when preparing for exams. As long as you are able to identify the few differences between the two actions, then you can consider them together – action taken in the CJEU can sometimes include both an Article 263 and an Article 265 action at the same time, because an Institution which has acted inappropriately can also be seen to have failed to act if in acting, it has missed out an essential procedure.

Defining its position

An Institution that has failed to act may not necessarily be required to do so under Article 265. It can merely 'define its position'. This basically means that it can produce a justification or explanation as to why it has not acted. You should bear in mind that a case against an Institution which has failed to act will not therefore automatically compel them to act, unless the only appropriate response from them is to do so. This therefore weakens the potential effect of this part of judicial review.

■ The consequences: Articles 263 and 265 TFEU

Where an action is successful in either Article 263 or 265, the consequence is the same: Article 266 states that the Institution must 'comply with the judgment of the Court of Justice'.

■ Putting it all together

Answer guidelines

See the essay question at the start of the chapter.

Approaching the question

Consider what this question is asking you. It requires you to focus specifically upon the rules regarding non-privileged applicants, particularly how they may have changed since the Lisbon Treaty came into effect. As we have discussed in this chapter, the requirements for private persons who wish to take action under Articles 263 and 265 are much more restrictive than for the Institutions and Member States. You therefore need to consider carefully the restrictions placed on individuals that you will not find placed on other applicants, and this will require you to contrast the two categories. You will also need to ensure that you are clear on how Article 263 TFEU has changed from the old Article 230 EC.

Important points to include

This question is asking you to consider two issues:

■ First, the way in which private persons are restricted, through the requirements in the Treaty; that the measure is either addressed to that person, of direct and individual concern to them, or a regulatory Act of direct concern to them. In particular, direct and individual concern has been narrowly interpreted through the use of the phrase 'fixed, closed class'. Look at the key cases such as *Plaumann* and *International Fruit*, and how they have interpreted the meaning of this. Comment on the effect this has had on a private individual's right to bring an action. ▶

■ Secondly, consider *why* the CJEU has been this restrictive in interpreting the Treaty. The *Codorniu* case shows some of the policy arguments behind the way it has interpreted the idea of class. Think about the potential problems of overloading the courts with actions, for example. You also need to consider the other cases listed in this chapter which have shown a more flexible approach to this issue.

■ In addition, consider why Article 263 is so restrictive. There are other avenues open to individuals who wish to object to an Act of the EU – Article 267 allows references to the CJEU on grounds of validity of an Act, for example, and the way in which an Act is applied in national courts can be defined through the direct effects rules in national courts.

■ However, you also need to consider the effect the Lisbon Treaty has had upon the operation of Articles 263 and 265. Arguably there is a broader approach here because the concept of 'Act' under Article 263 is wider than that of 'decision' under the old Article 230. There is also the new category of 'Regulatory Act' which has a less complicated requirement placed upon non-privileged applicants – although remember the definition applied to 'regulatory Acts' – non-legislative and of general application.

■ Your answer should show an appreciation of the way in which the law has changed and developed, through (a) the case law that has provided the important principles here, and also (b) the Treaty changes that have occurred through the Lisbon Treaty. This will allow you to demonstrate understanding of the way in which the rules operate, and not just knowledge of what those rules are.

 Make your answer stand out

This is an area of law that is heavily based upon the cases. There are many cases which provide good examples of the operation of this rule, for example where they are part of a fixed, closed class (such as Case C-152/88 *Sofrimport*), or where they have taken part in making the legislation (such as Case T-585/93 *Stichtig Greenpeace*), or restrictions on trade associations (such as Cases T-447–449/93 *AITEC*). You can make your answer stand out by your use of cases which show the CJEU's development of the law in this area, in particular when considering the post-Lisbon situation, and going beyond merely looking at the most significant cases here. On the issue of Lisbon, also bear in mind that much of the case development is being incorporated into the TFEU in Articles 263 and 265. Have a look at the wording of the old Articles 230 and 232 and you will see how the Treaty has been subtly redrafted. An understanding of recent developments in this area, like in the *Inuit* and *Microban* cases, are also a good way to show the examiner that you are up-to-date with relevant law.

READ TO IMPRESS

Albors-Llorens, A. (2003) 'The Standing of Private Parties to Challenge Community Measures: Has the European Court Missed the Boat?' 62 CLJ 72

Albors-Llorens, A. (2012) 'Remedies Against the EU Institutions After Lisbon: An Era of Opportunity?' 71 CLJ 507

Arnull, A. (2001) 'Private Applicants and the Action for Annulment since *Codorniu*', 38 CMLR 7

Cooke, J. (1997) '*Locus Standi* of Private Parties Under Article 173(4)', 6 IJEL 4

Craig, P. (1994) 'Legality, Standing and Substantive Review in Community Law', 14 OJLS 507

www.pearsoned.co.uk/lawexpress

Go online to access more revision support including quizzes to test your knowledge, sample questions with answer guidelines, podcasts you can download, and more!

Article 267 TFEU

Preliminary rulings in the CJEU

5

Revision checklist

Essential points you should know:

☐ The purpose behind the Article 267 reference procedure and its use

☐ Who may make a reference to the CJEU for interpretation

☐ The powers of a national court in making a reference and what must be done with it once received from the CJEU

☐ Obligations of a national court in circumstances where a reference is compulsory

☐ The CJEU's powers in dealing with a matter referred to it by a national court

■ Topic map

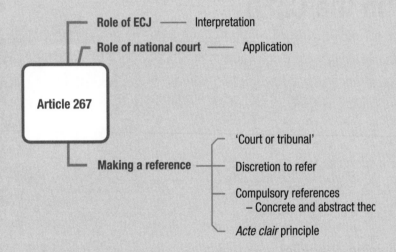

■ Introduction

Article 267 TFEU deals with references made to the Court of Justice of the European Union (CJEU) on matters of interpretation of European Union law.

(Please refer to Chapter 2 for an explanation of the CJEU (formerly ECJ).) This part of the CJEU's jurisdiction differs from other aspects of its work primarily because Article 267 references are not cases that the CJEU is dealing with directly, but instead are those dealt with by a national court, which will refer questions to the CJEU, and therefore the CJEU's role will not be one of decision-making, but predominantly interpretation.

Article 267 is important because of the consistency of interpretation that it provides. It is important that the rules are applied consistently, regardless of where in the EU that is. The procedure is a cooperative one, between the CJEU and the national courts of Member States. In this procedure, the CJEU provides the interpretation, and the national court is then given the responsibility to apply that interpretation to the case (Figure 5.1). This ensures that a consistent approach to interpretation of EU law is maintained, and it creates a clear link between national law and EU law.

Figure 5.1

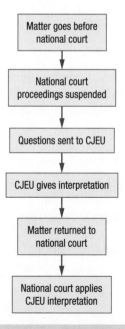

In assessments, you must always be aware of the division of roles in this procedure – each court has an important part to play, and neither court is considered to be in a superior position to the other – there is no hierarchy here, unlike in traditional relationships between courts. Therefore, questions can arise which focus upon the relationship between the national court and CJEU in this procedure, or on the respective roles of each court.

ASSESSMENT ADVICE

When Article 267 is the sole area examined in a question, it will commonly be dealt with as an essay, although it may also form part of a question which touches on other areas as well.

Essay questions

Both essay and problem questions can focus upon the relationship between the national court and CJEU generally, or concentrate upon one aspect of the procedure. The development of the principles surrounding the issue of what a court of last instance constitutes, or discussion of the *CILFIT* principle (see Case 283/81 *CILFIT and Others* v *Ministro della Sanità* [1982] ECR 3415) which gives us criteria where a national court may decline the opportunity to make a reference to the CJEU, are both examples which have been used in the past. The *CILFIT* principle and the case it is from are explained later in this chapter.

Problem questions

Article 267's relevance to wider topics can often appear in problem questions concerning cases before national courts – there can be an argument for making a reference to the CJEU as part of the issues raised by the problem.

■ Sample question

Could you answer this question? Below is a typical essay question that could arise on this topic. Guidelines on answering the question are included at the end of this chapter, whilst a sample problem question and guidance on tackling it can be found on the companion website.

ESSAY QUESTION

The decision of the High Court in *Arsenal Football Club* v *Reed* [2001] 2 CMLR 23 illustrates very well that the procedure set out in Article 267 is not an appeals procedure. It was intended to ensure the full collaboration of the municipal courts and the CJEU. This was in order to better develop and enforce EU law in an atmosphere of mutual regard for their relative jurisdictions.

Examine the extent to which this statement correctly states the purpose underlying Article 267.

The Article 267 procedure

KEY STATUTE

Article 267 TFEU

The Court of Justice shall have jurisdiction to give preliminary rulings concerning:

- the interpretation of this Treaty;
- the validity and interpretation of Acts of the Institutions, bodies, offices or agencies of the Union.

Where such a question is raised before any court or tribunal of a Member State, that court or tribunal may, if it considers that a decision on the question is necessary to enable it to give judgment, request the Court to give a ruling thereon.

Where any such question is raised in a case pending before a court or tribunal of a Member State against whose decisions there is no judicial remedy under national law, that court or tribunal shall bring the matter before the Court of Justice.

If such a question is raised in a case pending before a court or tribunal of a Member State with regard to a person in custody, the Court of Justice of the European Union shall act with the minimum of delay.

! Don't be tempted to . . .

Article 267 was referred to as Article 177 previously, and then Article 234 under the Amsterdam renumbering of the Treaty. Cases will refer to the number that was relevant at the time of the case, and it is therefore important to remember this when reading the judgments of these cases. You will need to refer to the new Article's number, so be careful not to get confused. If you cite an old Article number without any reference to the new numbering, expect to get picked up on it by your examiners.

The text of Article 267 is very similar to that of the text of the old Article 234, although the key difference is in one word: 'Acts'. This means the types of EU legislation upon which the CJEU may give a ruling is broader than before. This is in line with the broader concept of 'Act' that was discussed with regard to judicial review (in Chapter 4). There is one new section at the end of Article 267 which requires speedy action if the matter relates to someone in custody, and it should be fairly obvious as to why the inclusion of this was a good idea.

◾ Role of the Court of Justice of the European Union

The principle underlying the Article 267 procedure is cooperation between the CJEU and the courts of Member States. The CJEU has an important role to play in this, providing a consistent interpretation of matters of European law which is then uniformly applied throughout the EU. The CJEU can answer questions on:

- interpretation of the Treaties (TFEU, TEU);
- validity/interpretation of Acts of the Institutions.

It is important to emphasise that the jurisdiction of the CJEU extends no further than the answering of questions put to it by national courts – it cannot proactively deal with matters itself under a strict policy of non-interference. Once it has answered questions put to it, it cannot involve itself with the application of those answers; see *Arsenal Football Club* v *Reed* [2001] 2 CMLR 23 below.

◾ Powers of the Court of Justice of the European Union to answer questions

The CJEU has powers to deal with any questions of interpretation that are laid before it by a national court under this procedure. It does not choose the questions, and it cannot influence national courts in their choice of questions. It does, however, have the power to decide that questions are invalid. It can do so on various grounds. Some examples are shown in the table opposite.

As it stands, the CJEU is the only court that hears Article 267 cases. The Statute of the Court of Justice had previously laid down the possibility for the Court of First Instance (now the General Court) to also hear such cases (this was added by the Nice Treaty) and there is a mechanism for review of those cases should any be heard by the General Court, to create an appellate system between the General Court and the CJEU.

The boundary between the power of the CJEU and the power of the national court

The use of Article 267 is intended to be cooperative in nature, and therefore it is clear that the CJEU interprets, and the national court applies. However, there have been areas where overlap has occurred, causing friction.

Requirement of a question	Example
The question must be necessary for the national court to be able to give judgment	See Case 13/68 *Salgoil SA* v *Italian Minister of Foreign Trade* [1968] ECR 453
The question must not be a hypothetical one	See Case 244/80 *Foglia* v *Novello (No. 2)* [1981] ECR 3045, where the ECJ (now CJEU) refused a reference on the grounds that the proceedings had created an artificial situation in order to have a question answered
The CJEU may select which questions to answer	See Case 6/64 *Costa* v *ENEL* [1964] ECR 585
The CJEU may not rewrite questions	
The referring case must still be active	In order for the ruling to be meaningful, the case must not have been decided before the matter reaches the CJEU – therefore cases are suspended while a reference is made

---

KEY CASE

Arsenal Football Club v *Reed* [2001] 2 CMLR 23

Concerning: reference to ECJ (now CJEU); interpretation of EU law; duty of national court to follow ECJ (now CJEU) ruling

Facts

The *Arsenal* case concerned a reference made to the ECJ (now CJEU) asking several questions on the interpretation of the First Trade Marks Directive 89/104/EC. The case concerned Arsenal suing a seller of unofficial Arsenal merchandise (scarves, replica shirts, etc.) in defence of its registered trade mark in the Arsenal logo that appears on all its merchandise. The referral was made because the UK law on trade marks is based on the Trade Marks Directive. ▶

Legal principle

In answering the questions laid down by the High Court, the ECJ (now CJEU) also made comments that Laddie J considered to be applying the principles to the facts, which he believed to be outside the powers of the Court of Justice under Article 234 (now Article 267). He therefore applied what he saw as the interpretation, and disregarded anything he considered to be application to the facts. Although his decision was subsequently overturned by the Court of Appeal, the principle still, in theory, stands – it is not the place of the CJEU to decide the case, but to provide the interpretation to allow the national court to do this.

 Make your answer stand out

Because the *Arsenal* case was overruled by the Court of Appeal, the principle (above) isn't given very much gravity – however, the principle is an important one, and goes to the heart of the Article 267 procedure. The CJEU must not overstep its role in this procedure to the detriment of the national court's sovereignty. It must stick to interpretation, and not engage in applying the law to the facts. The importance of the CJEU's contribution is in the interpretation, as it is recognised that in order to ensure consistency of application of EU law, that the European Courts be responsible for the interpretation of EU law.

See Saunders (2004). The significance of this judgment is broader than it at first appears – you can show that you understand the general principle presented by this case, that the CJEU must not overstep the boundaries of what it is entitled to do under this procedure.

There are several different types of Article 267 procedure (see the following table) which have been introduced in order to speed up the procedure, which is infamous for the length of time it usually takes.

Procedure	Description
Simplified procedure	Where the questions referred are identical to previous questions and the answers can be deduced from existing case law
Accelerated procedure	Where the national court makes request on grounds of exceptional urgency
Urgent preliminary ruling procedure	For questions in the area of freedom, security and justice. Limited written procedure, case mostly dealt with electronically

■ Who may make a reference to the CJEU?

Article 267 refers to 'any **court or tribunal**'. This is not clearly defined, but subsequent cases have provided details as to what this means. Obviously the courts in the main judicial system would fall within this definition, but there are also many other tribunals that may wish to refer issues to the CJEU.

KEY DEFINITION: Court or tribunal

A court or tribunal should:

- ■ have a judicial function;
- ■ have independence from the parties concerned; and
- ■ be recognised by the state for its decision-making function.

This is a matter of EU law – it does not matter whether the Member State recognises the body as a court, if the EU recognises it as such. Also look at the *Broekmeulen* case below for further information.

The key elements of what the EU considers to be a court or tribunal are:

- ■ independence from the parties;
- ■ performance of a judicial function;
- ■ permanence.

You should bear in mind that the Member State may not consider a body to be a court or tribunal, but that does not matter, as long as the CJEU considers it to be one. This is one of a number of examples of where the CJEU will apply its own definition to a situation.

KEY CASE

Case 246/80 *Broekmeulen* v *Huisarts Registratie Commissie* [1981] ECR 2311

Concerning: definition of 'court or tribunal'

Facts

This case concerned the Dutch medical association responsible for registering doctors in the Netherlands. The committee was the appeals committee for the Society, usually regarding the registration of a doctor to practise in the Netherlands. It dealt with cases which had already been through another judicial committee of the Society. Although this was a private body, registration was important because it was not possible to practise medicine in that country without this registration. Broekmeulen had appealed to this committee when his registration to practise was refused. In dealing with his case, a reference to the ECJ (now CJEU) was made, and the issue as to whether the appeals committee was a 'court or tribunal' for the purposes of European law. ▶

> **Legal principle**
>
> The ECJ (now CJEU) decided that the appeals committee was a court or tribunal, despite the fact that Dutch law did not recognise it as such, because, as the CJEU said, it 'operates with the consent of the public authorities and their cooperation, and . . . after an adversarial procedure, delivers decisions which are recognised as final'. It therefore had all the necessary qualities that the court thought necessary for a body to be considered a court or tribunal for the purposes of EU law.

Exclusions

There are a couple of specific exclusions – domestic tribunals and arbitrators.

Domestic tribunals

The element that was missing from Case 138/80 *Re Jules Borker* [1980] ECR 1975, for example, was its recognition by the public authorities. This case concerned a committee of the Paris Bar Association, and, in refusing the reference, the ECJ (now CJEU) decided that it was 'not handling a lawsuit which it has the statutory function to decide'.

Arbitrators

Arbitrators are often not recognised as a 'court or tribunal' because parties have usually volunteered to refer their case to arbitration rather than being compelled to do so. For example, Case 102/81 *Nordsee Hochseefischerei GmbH* [1982] ECR 1095 was one where the procedure was **adversarial** in nature, just like the *Broekmeulen* case above. However, because the parties had previously agreed that in the event of a dispute they would go to the arbitrator (rather than the courts), then the Court of Justice decided that it was not a 'court or tribunal'. This was a private agreement, so the 'public' element was missing, therefore it wasn't a court – the state recognition aspect of the definition was absent.

✎ EXAM TIP

Although it may seem to be an obvious definition when answering a problem question, it is important to be able to establish definitively that a particular court or tribunal falls within the definition under Article 267, especially as this differs from national ideas of 'court or tribunal'. Don't assume that the examiner will consider this issue obvious. It is much better for you to discuss the issue to show that you have understood how it has been applied by the CJEU.

■ National courts' discretion to refer

When questions are raised in national courts which concern EU law, the national court has a choice whether to refer to the CJEU. The Treaty puts it as follows:

KEY STATUTE

Article 267(2) TFEU

Where such a question is raised before any court or tribunal of a Member State, that court or tribunal may, if it considers that a decision on the question is necessary to enable it to give judgment, request the Court to give a ruling thereon.

The decision to refer a matter to the CJEU for interpretation lies with the national court. It cannot be compelled to make a reference, either by the parties concerned or the CJEU itself, in a situation where Article 267(2) applies.

Any reference made by a national court, however, must be one genuinely needed for the case in hand. For example:

KEY CASE

Commissioners of Customs & Excise v *Samex Aps* [1983] 3 CMLR 194
Concerning: appropriateness of reference to CJEU; questions to raise

Facts

This case concerned the High Court's attempts to deal with European Regulations concerning an import licence that one of the parties, an acrylic yarn importer, was attempting to secure. In its deliberations, the court discussed the appropriateness of a reference to the ECJ (now CJEU), and what questions would be in order.

Legal principle

Bingham J pointed out in this case that where a party was attempting to use an Article 267 reference as a delaying tactic, this would justify the court's refusal to make a reference to the ECJ (now CJEU). This could otherwise be a delaying tactic, based upon the lengthy time it takes a reference to go through the Article 267 process. The other party would meanwhile be denied a remedy in the matter.

There are several other things to remember for discretionary references:

■ It is unimportant when the reference is made, as long as the case is still active – see Case 35/76 *Simmenthal* v *Amministrazione delle Finanze dello Stato* [1976] ECR 1871. Courts will usually make a preliminary judgment in which they will conclude with the questions they wish to address to the CJEU, and then make final judgment once the reference has been returned to them from the CJEU with their answers to the questions.

- Although the national court does not *have* to make a reference, it will need to clearly explain why, if it is not doing so – see Case 244/80 *Foglia* v *Novello* [1981] ECR 3045.

National court compulsory references

There are some circumstances where a national court has to refer questions to the CJEU. As stated in the Treaty:

KEY STATUTE

Article 267(3) TFEU

Where any such question is raised in a case pending before a court or tribunal of a Member State against whose decisions there is no judicial remedy under national law, that court or tribunal shall bring the matter before the Court.

In other words:

- if there is no right of appeal, and
- there are questions of EU law that need to be answered, then
- the national court *must* **make a reference** to the CJEU.

KEY DEFINITION: Making a reference

A national court makes a reference to the CJEU by putting together a list of questions for interpretation and submitting them for the CJEU to consider and provide interpretation.

Article 267(3) places an obligation on certain courts to make a reference to the CJEU in certain circumstances. Where a question is raised in a court where it is not possible to appeal, then that question must be referred under the Article 267 procedure. Such a court is referred to as a '**court of last instance**'.

KEY DEFINITION: Court of last instance

A court of last instance is the last court in a particular court structure to which cases can go. Therefore, this means that once the case has been heard by this court, there is no route of appeal to another court. The Supreme Court, as the highest court in England and Wales, is the best example of a court in the UK court system that will *always* come under this definition.

There have been two approaches to this issue:

Concrete theory	Abstract theory
The court of last instance is one from which there is no appeal in this *case*	The court of last instance is the only one from which there is never an appeal from this court

! Don't be tempted to . . .

It is important that you clearly understand the difference between *concrete* and *abstract* theory. The abstract theory was initially favoured by the UK judiciary – see Lord Denning's judgment in *Bulmer* v *Bollinger* [1974] Ch 401, because this meant only the House of Lords fell under an *obligation* to refer questions to the ECJ (now CJEU); however, the CJEU favoured the concrete theory, as shown in Case 6/64 *Costa* v *ENEL*, whereby if the case at hand cannot be appealed to a higher court then Article 267(3) applies. The UK judiciary ultimately changed their view so that they accepted the CJEU's approach. Agreement with this approach from judges in the UK can be seen in *Hagen* v *Fratelli* [1980] 3 CMLR 253 at 255.

✎ EXAM TIP

The issues surrounding the concrete vs the abstract theories have now been settled, and the UK judges have fallen into line with the thinking of the CJEU, in using the concrete theory (concerning appeal in this *case*). However, as the development of this procedure can be important in any discussion in an essay question, it is still vital for you to understand it, particularly as Article 267 is still split into mandatory and discretionary references. Being able to discuss the way in which mandatory references are defined can also be an important part of answering a problem question on this area.

The exception to Article 267(3): the *CILFIT* principle

KEY CASE

Case 283/81 *CILFIT and others* v *Ministero Della Sanità* [1982] ECR 3415

Concerning: justification for refusal to make a reference to the ECJ (now CJEU) under the Article 267 procedure

Facts

The facts of this case do not aid an understanding of the legal principle. ▶

Legal principle

This case considered whether there would be circumstances under which it would not be necessary to make a reference, even where there were questions of EU law, and the matter was in a court of last instance. The Court considered that it would not be necessary (under Art. 267(3)) to make a reference where:

- the question of EU law is irrelevant;
- the provision has already been interpreted by the ECJ (now CJEU);
- the correct application of EU law is so obvious as to leave no room for reasonable doubt.

This case shows that it is still down to the national court to make the reference, and still within its power to find grounds on which to refuse to make a reference. The *CILFIT* criteria listed in the above case box are still rather strict though, and therefore they serve to ensure that where the CJEU's opinion does not need to be sought, then the national court does not need to do so.

◼ The *acte clair* principle

In certain circumstances, the national court may be justified in refusing to make a reference to the CJEU. This is of particular significance if the court would otherwise be considered to be a court of last instance under Article 267(3). Such a refusal may be justified under the principle of *acte clair*.

KEY DEFINITION: *Acte clair*

Acte clair is a term borrowed from French administrative law. This phrase literally means that the law is clear or not in need of interpretation. If something is *acte clair*, then there is no reason to ask for clarification from the CJEU, and no question for the CJEU to answer.

The application of this principle can be seen through the cases. For example:

KEY CASE

Cases 28–30/62 *Da Costa en Schaake NV* v *Nederlandse Belastingadministratie* **[1963] ECR 31**

Concerning: acte clair

Facts

This case concerned a request for a reference to the ECJ (now CJEU) of questions which were virtually identical to those that had already been referred in the *Van Gend en Loos* case, and therefore the national court had to decide whether it was appropriate to make a reference in this case too.

Legal principle

The court decided in this case that if a question is almost identical to one which had already been answered by the ECJ (now CJEU) under the Article 267 procedure, then this will 'deprive the obligation [to refer] of its purpose and thus empty it of its substance'. In this circumstance, it would therefore be unnecessary for a national court to make a reference – the answer to their question could be found in the previous ruling of the CJEU.

KEY CASE

R v *Henn & Darby* [1978] 1 WLR 1031

Concerning: application of acte clair *principle*

Facts

This case concerned whether a ban on the import of pornographic materials was a quantitative restriction contrary to Article 28 of the EC Treaty (now Art. 34 TFEU). The court considered whether reference to the ECJ (now CJEU) under Article 267 was necessary.

Legal principle

The Court of Appeal decided against making a reference, as previous ECJ case law suggested that this would not be a quantitative restriction under what is now Article 34. However, when it reached the House of Lords, they did make a reference, and the ECJ decided that it *was* a quantitative restriction. The House of Lords warned about being too keen to decide that something was obvious, and therefore *acte clair*.

✎ EXAM TIP

There is considerable overlap between the *CILFIT* criteria and the *acte clair* principle in their application, although it is important not to confuse the two. *Acte clair* is more straightforward, as it merely refers to an issue of obviousness, whereas the *CILFIT* criteria are more specific and also include the ability not to refer, even where it's a relevant question, but where it has already been answered before. In a situation involving a question over whether a reference is necessary or not, it is important to explore both of these principles in order to show that you are familiar with both concepts and when they apply.

■ Proceedings after the reference

Once the CJEU has answered the questions put to it under Article 267, the matter returns to the national court. It is important to consider the following:

- The national court is under an obligation to follow the guidance of the CJEU and apply it to the case at hand (Member States have a general obligation under Article 4(3) of the TEU to give effect to EU law in general – a broad obligation that covers this).
- The case must therefore still be active until the matter returns from the CJEU.
- The national court applies the ruling to the facts. It is not the role of the CJEU to do this instead (see *Arsenal FC* v *Reed* [2001] 2 CMLR 23).

📖 REVISION NOTE

Remember: when it comes to applying the interpretation after the CJEU has dealt with the case, it is an issue of EU law that has been discussed. This is where questions on Article 267 overlap with other areas of *substantive* EU law. The free movement areas, or competition law, are good examples of where this can be the case. You would need to bring in your knowledge of these substantive areas alongside the procedure you have been discussing under Article 267.

■ Putting it all together

Answer guidelines

See the essay question at the start of the chapter.

Approaching the question

This question asks you to consider the effectiveness of Article 267 as a cooperative procedure between the national courts and the CJEU, and its effectiveness in dealing with issues of EU law. It is a very open question, but allows you to demonstrate a clear and detailed understanding of this area of EU law. You therefore need to consider examples from cases which may provide you with points about the cooperative nature of Article 267, as well as bearing in mind the nature of the procedure itself. Note also that, ultimately, this question requires you to consider the underlying purpose of the Article 267 procedure, so think about what it is intended to achieve.

Important points to include

It is important to:

- Be able to show an understanding of the Article 267 procedure, and the roles of the national court and the CJEU in it.
- Discuss any conflicts between the CJEU and the national courts in relevant case law, in particular the problems encountered in the *Arsenal* case, but also consider other ways in which the national courts and the CJEU might have overlap or conflict in the operation of the Article 267 procedure.
- Discuss the advantages of this system for the interpretation and application of EU law.
- Discuss the purpose of the procedure – remember this is predominantly for the interpretation and validity of Acts of the EU.
- Consider other avenues for the examination of EU law that exist – the use of judicial review under Articles 263 and 265, for example.

 Make your answer stand out

This question is one which calls for more than mere reproduction of memorised facts about the Article 267 procedure, and therefore you need to use what you know about the procedure and issues raised by it to create an analytical discussion of the procedure and its purpose in the EU legal system. Show that your comprehension stretches beyond just what the relevant cases are and what they say – make your answer an integrated discussion of the topic as a whole, and you will show that you really do understand this area, and haven't just memorised a load of 'stuff' to blurt out in your examination answer.

Also, show that you understand the context within which this procedure sits, and therefore the importance of the cooperative aspect of this procedure in order to ensure that EU law is dealt with consistently.

READ TO IMPRESS

Mance, J. (2013) 'The Interface Between National and European Law', 38 EL Rev 437

Saunders, O. (2004) 'A Warning Shot Across the Bows of the ECJ: The Lessons of *Arsenal Football Club* v *Reed*', *Legal Executive Journal* 38

Tridimas, T. (2003) 'Knocking on Heaven's Door: Fragmentation, Efficiency and Defiance in the Preliminary Reference Procedure', 40 CMLR 9

www.pearsoned.co.uk/lawexpress

Go online to access more revision support including quizzes to test your knowledge, sample questions with answer guidelines, podcasts you can download, and more!

Free movement of goods part 1

Taxes, duties and charges

6

Revision checklist

Essential points you should know:

☐ The rules promoting free movement of goods in the EU through the prohibition of taxes, duties and charges

☐ How those rules have evolved in the Court of Justice of the EU

☐ The types of measures taken by national governments which will be prohibited by the rules

☐ How that applies to individual cases

■ Topic map

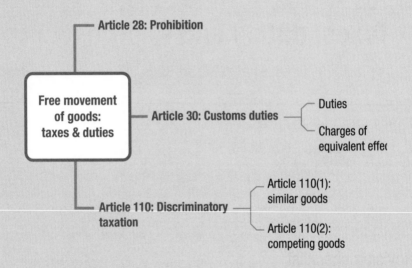

- **Article 28: Prohibition**

Free movement of goods: taxes & duties

- **Article 30: Customs duties**
  - Duties
  - Charges of equivalent effe(

- **Article 110: Discriminatory taxation**
  - Article 110(1): similar goods
  - Article 110(2): competing goods

A printable version of this topic map is available from **www.pearsoned.co.uk/lawexpress**

■ Introduction

Free movement of goods is central to the existence of the European Single Market.

Without this freedom, an important part of the internal EU structure is missing. In order to achieve the free movement of **goods**, the EU has placed restrictions upon individual States' ability to affect the movement of goods across national boundaries through taxation. This therefore means restrictions on both imports and exports. In order to address all the different ways that Member States might be tempted to affect this free flow of goods between the States, the EU has two basic rules concerning the movement of goods between Member States:

- There must not be any tariffs or charges imposed on goods moving between Member States
- There must not be restrictions affecting quantities of goods moving between Member States

where goods are being moved from one EU country to another.

In this chapter, we are going to look at the first of these bullet points, regarding taxation. The EU rules are also intended to catch anything which, although not an obvious charge on goods, *has the same effect* as one, and this is also a very important aspect of the law in this area.

This area is covered mainly by Articles 28–30, although there is a wealth of case law which has developed as a result of the ECJ's (now CJEU's) discussion of what is covered by the free movement rules, and what can be justified. This chapter will examine the development of the law from the Treaty through the cases, as often the issues to be discussed in an answer to either an essay-style question or a problem question require an understanding of the rules and how they have developed.

ASSESSMENT ADVICE

Essay questions

An essay question on this subject would usually ask you to analyse the rules from the Treaties through the cases, and therefore would require you to have a good knowledge of the relevant case law in this area. It may ask you to discuss the issues generally, or it may centre on a particular issue, for example the meaning of a charge equivalent to a customs duty. In any event it will require some form of analysis of case law, and ▶

therefore merely reiterating the principles from the cases will not suffice. You need to acquire a good understanding of how the law has developed through the cases.

Problem questions

A problem question in this area is likely to be one which can overlap with other areas of EU law. For example, one common overlap can be with the Article 258 action, because if a Member State is in contravention of Article 30, this can also be the basis of an enforcement action by the European Commission under Article 258 (see Chapter 3). Alternatively the question may be one involving a company pursuing an action in the domestic courts, in which case there may also be issues of direct effect such as those seen in the *Van Gend en Loos* case (see Chapter 1). In any event, a problem question will require you to analyse the situation and decide how to apply the rules and definitions relevant to that area.

■ Sample question

Could you answer this question? Below is a typical problem question that could arise on this topic. Guidelines on answering the question are included at the end of this chapter, whilst a sample essay question and guidance on tackling it can be found on the companion website.

PROBLEM QUESTION

Sebastian is an importer of widgets into France for the automotive industry. He imports exclusively from other EU countries, where widget manufacture is more common than in France. He has incurred a number of charges recently, and is seeking advice from you regarding the following matters:

The French authorities have placed a quality inspection requirement on all widgets imported from other EU States, after some high-profile car crashes in the EU involving French-built cars manufactured with cheap imported widgets. The importer is charged a fee for each inspection carried out by the French authorities. Given the long-held reputation of quality of the French-produced widget, the same inspection requirement and charge is not placed upon widgets produced in France.

Each crate of imported widgets is levied a charge on entry to France, which is paid into the Widget Workers' Benevolent Fund, intended to tackle issues of poverty amongst workers in widget factories in all parts of the EU.

Advise Sebastian as to whether he has grounds in EU law to object to any of the above.

■ Free movement of goods under the TFEU

The principle of free movement of goods can be found in Articles 28–37 of the TFEU. However, this chapter concentrates on Articles 28 and 30, and the next chapter concentrates on Articles 34–36. This is where the main focus of this area lies, both in EU law courses and in assessments, as the Articles in this chapter cover the prohibitions on tariffs, and the Articles in Chapter 7 cover quantitative restrictions and derogations.

KEY STATUTE

Article 28 TFEU

The Union shall comprise a customs union which shall cover all trade in goods and which shall involve the prohibition between Member States of customs duties on imports and exports and of all charges having equivalent effect, and the adoption of a common customs tariff in their relations with third countries.

KEY DEFINITION: Goods

Goods are interpreted as 'products which can be valued in money and which are capable, as such, of forming the subject of commercial transactions' (Case 7/68 *Re Export Tax on Art Treasures: EC Commission* v *Italy* [1968] ECR 423 at 428).

Alternatively, goods are considered to be 'manufactured material objects' (Cases 60 & 61/84 *Cinéthèque*).

The main provisions concerning free movement of goods are as follows:

Treaty Article	Function
Article 30	Prohibition on customs duties and charges having an equivalent effect
Article 34	Elimination of quantitative restrictions on imports and measures having an equivalent effect (MEQRs)
Article 35	Elimination of quantitative restrictions on exports and measures having an equivalent effect (MEQRs)
Article 36	Derogations from Articles 34–35

We are going to look only at the first of these in this chapter – the remaining Articles will be dealt with in Chapter 7.

◼ Article 30 TFEU: customs union

Article 30 provides a **negative duty** on the Member States not to impose **customs duties**. Member States need not take any action under this Article, but must not impose any new duties on imports and exports.

KEY STATUTE

Article 30 TFEU

Customs duties on imports and exports and charges having equivalent effect shall be prohibited between Member States. This prohibition shall also apply to customs duties of a fiscal nature.

KEY DEFINITION: Negative duty

Many rules of EU law do not impose a duty to do something, but rather a duty NOT to do something – as seen here with Article 30, this is a negative duty.

For example, see *Van Gend en Loos* v *Nederlandse Administratie der Belastingen*. This is a case you should be familiar with (from Chapter 1) as it is also important for the area of direct effects of Treaty Articles. However, here it is important because it is a case about customs tariffs.

KEY CASE

Case 26/62 *Van Gend en Loos* v *Nederlandse Administratie der Belastingen* [1963] ECR 1

Concerning: the imposition of an increased customs duty upon goods being imported into the Netherlands

Facts

The goods in question were reclassified by the Dutch government so they became subject to a higher rate of duty. The importers attempted to use what is now Article 30 (but then it was Art. 12) to challenge the new duty in the national courts.

Legal principle

The ECJ (now CJEU) ruled that as the new duty imposed a higher rate of import duty upon the importer, it was a direct contravention of what is now Article 30, and that this Article provided a right which could be enforced by individual EU citizens.

KEY DEFINITION: Customs duties

Customs duties are those charges that are imposed at the point that goods cross a national boundary. Because of this they are an obstacle to goods moving from one EU country to another and are prohibited.

The prohibition under Article 30 is therefore absolute, and so, unlike Article 34, does not have the scope for Member States to justify charges. Also, the purpose of the charge is irrelevant – look at the following case regarding this:

KEY CASE

Case 7/68 *Commission* v *Italy – Re: Export Tax on Art Treasures* [1968] ECR 617

Concerning: justifications for imposing customs tariffs

Facts

This case concerned customs duties imposed by the Italian State upon certain cultural treasures and artefacts which, after having been sold to private collectors from outside Italy, were being shipped out of the country. The Italian authorities attempted to justify this by claiming that the charges were there in order to discourage people from taking such treasures out of Italy in order to preserve their cultural heritage.

Legal principle

The ECJ (now CJEU) ruled that the purpose of the export tax was irrelevant. The mere fact that the tax was prohibited by Article 30 was enough for Italy to be considered to be breaching EU law.

The key thing to remember here is that the prohibition is treated as absolute – there is nothing that can excuse what is, according to the letter of the law, a breach of Article 30. Even where there is no domestic product that might get an advantage from such a customs duty, customs duties are still prohibited (see Cases 2 & 3/69 *Sociaal Fonds voor de Diamondarbeiders*, where there was no domestic market for diamonds). The purpose behind the rule is to make the EU a single, unified market, with no obstacles in the way of anyone in the EU, regardless of where the goods are moving from, or to.

! Don't be tempted to . . .

You should remember that there are no defences that can excuse a breach of Article 30. This is in contrast to Articles 34 and 35 (see Chapter 7), which have a number of defences, from cases and from the TFEU itself (in the form of Article 36) that can excuse a breach of Article 34 or 35. Note also that these defences do **not** apply to Article 30. Don't get these two parts of free movement of goods law confused with each other.

Purpose of the charge

Where a customs charge is levied, the ECJ (now CJEU) has also pointed out that it is irrelevant what the purpose of that charge is. See for example:

KEY CASE

Cases 2 & 3/69 *Sociaal Fonds voor de Diamondarbeiders* **[1969] ECR 211**

Concerning: tariffs imposed for benevolent purposes

Facts

This case concerned a charge imposed on diamond imports into Belgium. The purpose of the charge was to provide a social fund for people working in Belgium in the diamond industry. It was challenged on the grounds that it was a customs duty.

Belgium argued that the prohibition of customs duties was intended to remove protectionism – and that because there was no domestic market for the production of diamonds, as well as the benevolent purpose of the charge, this should not be considered a breach of Article 30.

Legal principle

The ECJ (now CJEU) held that the effect of the charge, however small, charged at a border, would be an obstacle to the free movement of goods, regardless of the motivation for imposing it. This was therefore a breach of Article 30.

Charges equivalent to customs duties

As well as customs duties, which tend to be obvious as they are charges directly imposed at the time of import, there are also equivalent charges to consider. They are defined as follows:

KEY CASE

Case 24/68 *Commission* v *Italy* **[1969] ECR 193**

Concerning: definition of charges equivalent to customs duties

Facts

The Italian government placed a levy on statistical information because it constituted consideration for a business service.

Legal principle

In this case, the ECJ (now CJEU) defined charges equivalent to customs duties as follows:

> any pecuniary charge, however small and whatever its designation and mode of application, which is imposed unilaterally on domestic and foreign goods by reason of the fact that they cross a frontier . . .

This is therefore quite a wide definition, but the important part of this is the fact of something crossing a frontier. So charges for health inspections where they are only applied to imports would be considered to be a charge equivalent to a customs duty because it only applies to imports and it is triggered by the crossing of a frontier. Where these charges apply to both domestic and imported goods, then there may be an issue under Article 110 TFEU (see later in this chapter for details).

The limits of Article 30

Although customs duties are absolutely prohibited, there are some charges that are permitted, even though on the face of it they appear to be charges equivalent to a customs duty. These usually relate to additional requirements that goods go through when entering a State, and this is illustrated by the following case:

KEY CASE

Case 132/82 *Commission* v *Belgium* [1983] ECR 1649

Concerning: charges applied to imports which are not a breach of Article 30

Facts

The Belgian authorities placed a charge on goods being brought into the country at the point they passed through the customs inspection system. There were two aspects to this charge. One was a compulsory charge for storage which was for the period that goods were kept by the Belgian authorities for inspection; however, there was a second charge, which was optional. If the importers wished to keep their goods at the inspection warehouse for an additional period of time after the inspection took place before collecting them, they could do so, but they would be charged a storage fee.

Legal principle

The first charge was considered a charge equivalent to a customs duty because it was compulsory and applied to everyone. However, the second charge was not, because it was optional, and was in return for a *genuine service* – storage of goods until the importer collected them.

Ordinarily, charges for health inspections cannot be charged for. The reasoning behind this is that the health inspection is for the benefit of citizens in that State, and therefore the State should be responsible for paying for them. However, inspections which are required by the EU itself, can be charged for. See Case 18/87 *Commission* v *Germany*, which concerned livestock inspections required by Directive 81/389/EEC. As these inspections were required in the whole of the EU, the charge to the importer was not prohibited.

■ Discriminatory taxation: Article 110 TFEU

Charges which discriminate against imports may not always be charged at the point that goods enter the State, and therefore, to make sure that all charges that may unfairly re-partition the Single Market are removed, there is also Article 110. This Article differs from Articles 28–30 because it concerns charges imposed after the goods have already been imported, but it is still about their treatment because of the fact that they have been imported. Although this does not relate to the point that goods are imported, and therefore is not directly about import duties, it does close an important loophole that may otherwise allow Member States to favour their own products over those brought in from other EU Member States.

KEY STATUTE

Article 110 TFEU

No Member State shall impose, directly or indirectly, on the products of other Member States any internal taxation of any kind in excess of that imposed directly or indirectly on similar domestic products.

Furthermore, no Member State shall impose on the products of other Member States any internal taxation of such a nature as to afford indirect protection to other products.

This Article is designed to prevent protectionism through the way that the Member States organise their internal taxation, as this is something that is still dealt with by the Member States themselves. It takes a two-pronged approach:

- Prohibition on taxes which discriminate between imports and *similar* domestic goods.
- Prohibition on taxes which discriminate between imports and *competing* domestic goods.

It is intended to cover situations where there is tax imposed on imports, and there is either less tax on domestic products, or no tax at all. The tax is not imposed when the goods are imported, but further down the supply chain, or may be imposed upon the ultimate consumer. However, the principle is the same: the tax is higher because these are goods that originated from outside that Member State.

Article 110(1): similar goods

Goods will need to be objectively judged as 'similar' before any comparison on the amount of tax levied can be made.

KEY CASE

Case 243/84 *John Walker* v *Ministeriet for Skatter* [1986] ECR 875

Facts

The Court in this case had to decide whether liqueur fruit wine was similar to whisky. It examined various aspects of each of the products: alcohol content, methods of production, consumer perceptions.

Legal principle

When judging the similarity, this has to be done objectively on the different characteristics of the two products concerned. In this case, the difference in alcohol content and the fact that one was produced by fermenting, the other by distillation, meant that these were not similar products.

Even generic categories applied to products will not necessarily make them similar. Applying the above principle regarding characteristics of the product, the Court in Case 184/85 *Commission* v *Italy* [1987] ECR 2013 had to decide whether a generic categorisation of 'fruit' made all fruit similar. It was decided that the objective characteristics of bananas meant that they were not similar to other fruit for the purposes of Article 110. In this case the Court accepted that there were differences in different types of fruit that made them dissimilar enough not to be covered by Article 110(1).

! Don't be tempted to . . .

Don't look for any form of intention of the Member State to discriminate – this will often not be an obvious factor, and in some cases the discrimination may not be deliberate. Article 110 is more concerned with the effect of the tax, rather than seeking any motive.

For example, Case 112/84 *Humblot* v *Directeur des Services Fiscaux* [1985] ECR 1367 involved a taxation system imposed upon cars based on a number of factors regarding the car's engine and the size of different aspects of it. However, it just so happened that where a French-produced car fell into the lower tax band, the equivalent imported car fell into the higher tax band. This was still discriminatory, regardless of any intention or deliberate act of the French Government in imposing this tax.

Article 110(2): competing goods

The second paragraph of Article 110 deals with goods which, although not similar, do compete with each other. Look at the following two cases, which deal with the same point:

KEY CASE

Case 168/78 *Commission* v *France* [1980] ECR 347

Facts

The Court had to decide whether grain-based alcoholic products (such as whisky, rum, gin, etc.) competed with wine or fruit-based products (such as cognac, armagnac, wine, etc.). France produced far more of the fruit-based products, but the tax was higher on the grain-based products.

Legal principle

Despite not being 'similar' (see Case 243/84 *John Walker* v *Ministeriet for Skatter*) they did compete with each other because they may be considered alternative choices for people as alcoholic beverages.

KEY CASE

Case 170/78 *Commission* v *UK* [1983] ECR 2265

Facts

The Court in this case looked at the effect of the taxation difference between wines and beers. Just like the *Commission* v *France* case (above), these were considered to be competing products despite their differences. However, in the UK, more beers were produced than wines, and the tax was higher on the wines.

Legal principle

The effect of the difference in taxation of these competing products, as a result of the fact that the product with the lower tax was mainly produced domestically, and the product with the higher tax was predominantly imports, was discriminatory towards imports. The same conclusion was reached in the *Commission* v *France* case.

Therefore, the important issue here is whether:

1. the products compete; and
2. the effect of the tax difference is such that the domestic products are more favourably taxed than imports,

because ultimately this results in an internal barrier to the Single Market.

■ Putting it all together

Answer guidelines

See the problem question at the start of the chapter.

Approaching the question

This question asks you to advise an importer of products into France regarding the rules on taxes and duties on those imports. There are essentially two parts to this question, regarding the charge that is made for the inspection, and also the entry charge to be paid into the Widget Workers' Benevolent Fund. You need to discuss each of these issues separately, and make sure you do not mix up or confuse between the two – because some of the law you need to use may be common between these two issues.

Important points to include

An approach to this question could include the following points:

- The attempt by the authorities to charge for the inspection could be seen, not as a customs charge, but a charge having equivalent effect. You need to examine the effect that this charge has on imports, and in particular comment on the difference in the way domestic products are treated.

- This charge for inspection might be treated differently if it was an EU requirement; however, the question clearly shows this has come from the French government.

- The inspection itself might be a breach of Article 34 – you would need to look at Chapter 7 to determine whether this is the case – this does show how there can be overlap in such questions.

- The other charge, on the importation of widgets for the benevolent fund, should be considered as a possible customs charge – look at the definition in Article 30.

- Consider the effect of what the charge is for – does this justify it? See the *Sociaal Fonds voor de Diamondarbeiders* case mentioned earlier in this chapter. You need to remember the approach of the CJEU towards attempted justifications for breaches of Article 30 – see Case 7/68 *Commission* v *Italy (Re: Export Tax on Art Treasures)*. ▶

Make your answer stand out

Where you have been given a number of issues in a problem question like this, often examiners are trying to hint at possible cases to apply through the way in which they present their question. Remember examiners are not trying to catch you out, but to present you with opportunities to show your knowledge; so make sure you know the relevant cases and, where they are factually similar, be prepared to use them.

READ TO IMPRESS

Barents, R. (1978) 'Charges of Equivalent Effect to Customs Duties', 15 CMLR 415

Easoon, A. (1980) 'The Spirits, Wine and Beer Judgments: A Legal Mickey Finn?', 5 EL Rev 318

Kingston, S. (2006–7) 'The Boundaries of Sovereignty: The ECJ's Controversial Role Applying Internal Market Law to Direct Tax Measures', 9 CYELS 287

Snell, J. (2007) 'Non-Discriminatory Tax Obstacles in Community Law', 56 ICLQ 339

www.pearsoned.co.uk/lawexpress

 Go online to access more revision support including quizzes to test your knowledge, sample questions with answer guidelines, podcasts you can download, and more!

Free movement of goods part 2

Quantitative restrictions and MEQRs

Revision checklist

Essential points you should know:

- [ ] The rules governing restrictions or bans affecting free movement of goods in the EU
- [ ] How those rules have evolved in the Court of Justice
- [ ] The types of measures taken by national governments which will be prohibited by the rules
- [ ] How that applies to individual cases

■ Topic map

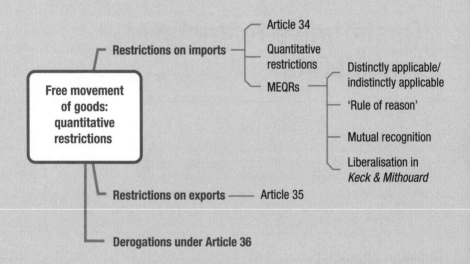

■ Introduction

Free movement of goods is central to the existence of the European Single Market.

Without this freedom, an important part of the internal EU structure is missing. In order to achieve the free movement of **goods**, the EU has placed restrictions upon individual States' ability to affect the movement of goods across national boundaries. This therefore means restrictions on both imports and exports. In order to address all the different ways that Member States might be tempted to affect this free flow of goods between the States, the EU has two basic rules concerning the movement of goods between Member States:

- There must not be restrictions affecting quantities of goods moving between Member States.
- There must not be any tariffs or charges imposed on goods moving between Member States.

where goods are being moved from one EU country to another.

We looked at the way in which taxes affected the free movement of goods in the last chapter, and this chapter will concentrate upon the quantitative restrictions and the rules regarding these, including justifications. The EU rules are also intended to catch anything which, although not an obvious charge or restriction on goods, *has the same effect* as one, and this is also a very important aspect of the law in this area. This is an area covered mainly by just three Treaty Articles, Articles 34–36, although there is a wealth of case law which has developed as a result of the ECJ's (now CJEU's) discussion of what is covered by the free movement rules, and what can be justified. This chapter will examine the development of the law from the Treaty through the cases, as often the issues to be discussed in an answer to either an essay-style question or a problem question require an understanding of the rules and how they have developed.

ASSESSMENT ADVICE

Essay questions

An essay question on this subject would usually ask you to analyse the concept of free movement of goods through the cases, and therefore would require you to have a good knowledge of the relevant case law in this area. It may ask you to discuss the issues generally, or it may centre on a particular issue, for example the rule of reason. Because the rules that come from cases in this area have evolved over a period of time, a question may expect you to be able to analyse the development through the ▶

case law. In any event it will require some form of analysis, and therefore merely reiterating the history of the cases will not suffice. You need to ensure that you have an *understanding* of the effect of the case law on this area, as it will allow you to deal with whatever question you may encounter in the examination.

Problem questions

A problem question in this area is likely to be one which can overlap with other areas of EU law. For example, one common overlap can be with the Article 258 action, because if a Member State is in contravention of Article 34 or 35, this can also be the basis of an enforcement action by the European Commission under Article 258 (see Chapter 3). Alternatively the question may be one involving a company pursuing an action in the domestic courts, in which case there may also be issues of direct effect (see Chapter 1). In any event, a problem question will require you to analyse the situation and decide what type of restriction is involved (tariff or quantitative restriction) and then apply the rules and definitions relevant to that area.

■ Sample question

Could you answer this question? Below is a typical essay question that could arise on this topic. Guidelines on answering the question are included at the end of this chapter, whilst a sample problem question and guidance on tackling it can be found on the companion website.

ESSAY QUESTION

Assess the importance of the decision in Case 120/78 *Rewe-Zentral AG* v *Bundesmonopolverwaltung für Branntwein (Cassis de Dijon)* [1979] ECR 649, and by reference to decided case law critically analyse the way in which the 'rule of reason' has subsequently been developed.

■ Free movement of goods under the TFEU

The principle of free movement of goods can be found in Articles 28–37 of the TFEU. However, this chapter concentrates on Articles 34–36, as this is where the main focus of this area lies, both in EU law courses and in assessments, as these Articles cover the prohibitions on quantitative restrictions and derogations from those restrictions.

KEY DEFINITION: Goods

See Chapter 6 for the definition of 'Goods' – this is applied in the same way here.

The main provisions concerning free movement of goods are as follows:

Treaty Article	Function
Article 30	Prohibition on customs duties and charges having an equivalent effect
Article 34	Elimination of quantitative restrictions on imports and measures having an equivalent effect (MEQRs)
Article 35	Elimination of quantitative restrictions on exports and measures having an equivalent effect (MEQRs)
Article 36	Derogations from Articles 34–35

As we have already looked at the relevant law regarding customs tariffs under Article 30 in the previous chapter, we will now concentrate on the other three Articles, regarding quantitative restrictions. Also note that, unlike Article 30, there are derogations that apply to Articles 34 and 35; this is because unlike with customs duties and tariffs, there are circumstances in which quantitative restrictions on goods by Member States may be justified. We will cover those at the end of this chapter.

Article 34 TFEU: restrictions on imports

Article 34 is the main provision because it deals with quantitative restrictions and equivalent measures affecting *imports*. Article 35 deals with exports but is much less significant because most of the issues arise from Member States attempting to restrict the flow of goods into their State, rather than out of it.

KEY STATUTE

Article 34 TFEU

Quantitative restrictions on imports and all measures having equivalent effect shall be prohibited between Member States.

! Don't be tempted to . . .

With the renumbering that occurred under the Treaty of Amsterdam, and then subsequently under the Treaty of Lisbon, Article 30 was renumbered Article 28 (and is now Art. 34) and Article 36 was renumbered Article 30 (and is now Art. 36 again!). This may cause confusion where cases refer to the *old* numbering system – bear this in mind when reading cases decided before the Treaties of Amsterdam and Lisbon came into effect.

Unlike Article 30, Articles 34 and 35 required Member States to take positive action to make sure free movement of goods is respected, as well as to refrain from taking action contrary to the principle.

Two types of measure are prohibited by Article 34:

- Quantitative restrictions on imports/exports.
- Measures having an equivalent effect to quantitative restrictions (MEQRs).

Quantitative restrictions

Quantitative restrictions are easily defined and therefore fairly uncontroversial. A quantitative restriction is one where imports or exports are either partially or totally restricted. This would include quota systems, bans, and can potentially also be any form of licensing system. Even where the application for an import licence is considered a mere formality, it can still be considered a quantitative restriction because it is a mechanism whereby imports can be restricted. A licensing system can have the potential to be a quantitative restriction, if through its application it limits the amount of goods that come into a Member State. However, even where the licensing system does not put specific limits on quantities of goods coming into a country, it may be considered to be a Measure Equivalent to a Quantitative Restriction (MEQR). It therefore sits in a grey area. Quantitative restrictions often breach Article 34 merely because of their effect – they discriminate against imported products, and therefore attract the accusation that they are a barrier to free trade between EU Member States. Because they are very straightforward, they are also rather rare, and have been pretty much eradicated from the EU.

MEQRs

MEQRs are wider in scope. They add complication to this area because they can be measures which apply to both domestic and imported products. However, it is their *effect* which is important. It is also important to remember that they may not have been intended to have the effect they have by the Member State that has put them in place. Although not defined by the Treaty, there are two definitions of MEQRs:

KEY CASE

Case 8/74 *Procureur du Roi* v *Dassonville* [1974] ECR 837 at 852

Concerning: definition of MEQR

Facts

This case involved a Belgian law which required certain products (such as Scotch whisky) to be sold only if they had a certificate of origin included with them. The traders involved in this case were prosecuted for selling Scotch Whisky without a certificate, but they had bought it from France, where no certificate was required. The issue was whether this requirement fell within Article 34 or not.

Legal principle

All trading rules enacted by Member States which are capable of hindering, directly or indirectly, actually or potentially, intra-Community trade.

The definition in the *Dassonville* case was very broad, and therefore meant that a lot of actions of the Member States could breach Article 34, even where they resulted from national differences and were as equally applicable to domestic products as they were to imports. This was a very generous definition which paid no attention to the *intention* of the government in question, but about the possible *effect* of the measure. Therefore, something could be categorised as an MEQR even if it only had the potential to affect trade, not that it actually did. Case C-249/81 *Commission* v *Ireland (Buy Irish)* [1982] ECR 4005 shows this. However, the purpose behind the *Dassonville* formula was preventing the EU being redivided along national borders by such measures. One major weakness of this definition is a lack of distinction between distinctly and **indistinctly applicable measures**. These however were defined in the following Directive:

KEY STATUTE

Directive 70/50/EEC Article 2(3)

Directive 70/50, Article 2(3) provides a non-exhaustive list of MEQRs, and subdivides them into:

- distinctly applicable measures (those which apply only to imported goods);
- indistinctly applicable measures (those which apply equally to imported goods and domestically produced goods).

The non-exhaustive list includes:

- laying down minimum and maximum sale prices;
- fixing import prices at less favourable levels than prices of domestic products;
- exclusion of prices for imports that reflect importation costs;
- requiring an agent to be used in order to access markets in the State being imported to;
- requiring payment or special conditions of imported products which are not required of domestic ones and are more difficult to satisfy;
- requiring imported goods to give guarantees or make payment on account, but not requiring the same of domestic products;
- subjecting only imported goods to conditions that are different from the ones required of domestic goods, e.g. size, weight, shape, etc., and which are more difficult to satisfy;

▶

- hindering purchase by consumers of domestic goods or giving preference to domestic goods;

- precluding importers (either partially or fully) from using national facilities or giving preference to domestic producers;

- prohibition or limitation of publicity for imported products, or preference given to publicity of domestic products.

Distinctly applicable measures

These are measures which apply *only* to imports/exports or goods in transit. It is therefore more straightforward to assess whether they breach Articles 34 and 35, because in assessing their effect on the market, it is more straightforward to show that their effect is to discriminate in favour of domestic products.

Indistinctly applicable measures

KEY DEFINITION: Indistinctly applicable measures

These are restrictions or other measures which apply equally to imported products and domestic products, for example Case 261/81 *Walter Rau Lebensmittelwerke* v *De Smedt PVBA* [1982] ECR 3961, where there was a requirement in Belgium for all margarine sold there to be contained in cube-shaped boxes, or the *Cassis de Dijon* case (see below) where all cassis sold in Germany was required to contain at least 25 per cent alcohol.

Because indistinctly applicable measures are those which apply to imports and domestic products, the approach of the CJEU towards them has been less strict. This is because, despite their potential to repartition the internal market, there are more likely to be valid mitigating reasons as to why these measures should be allowed. This formed the basis of the decision in the following case:

KEY CASE

Case 120/78 *Rewe-Zentral AG* v *Bundesmonopolverwaltung für Branntwein (Cassis de Dijon)* [1979] ECR 649

Concerning: indistinctly applicable measures and their validity under Article 34

Facts

A German law prohibited sale of various liquors (including cassis) in Germany with an alcohol content lower than 25 per cent. The claimants in this case attempted to import French cassis into Germany, which had an alcohol content of somewhere between 15 and 20 per cent.

Legal principle

The ECJ (now CJEU) introduced two principles to address the problems caused by its previous failure in the *Dassonville* case to distinguish between distinctly applicable and indistinctly applicable measures. These would allow exceptions whereby indistinctly applicable measures would not be subject to Article 28 (now Art. 34) and therefore allow those indistinctly applicable measures to stand. See below for a discussion of the two rules in *Cassis de Dijon*.

The first *Cassis* rule: the Rule of Reason

Restrictions would be allowed for *indistinctly* applicable measures if they could satisfy certain mandatory requirements, such as:

- effectiveness of fiscal supervision;
- protection of public health;
- fairness of consumer transactions;
- defence of the consumer.

Examples of this approach were discussed in the following cases:

Case	Exception under the rule of reason
Cases 60 & 61/84 *Cinéthèque SA* v *Fédération Nationale des Cinémas Françaises* [1985] ECR 2605	Protection of a Member State's culture
Case 302/86 *Commission* v *Denmark* [1988] ECR 4607	Protection of the environment
Case C-169/91 *Stoke-on-Trent City Council and Another* v *B & Q Plc* [1993] 1 CMLR 426	Socio-cultural characteristics of a country
Case 120/78 *Rewe-Zentral AG* v *Bundesmonopolverwaltung für Branntwein (Cassis de Dijon)* [1979] ECR 649	Protection of public health

The general rule appears to be that if a measure is necessary, then it can be allowed under the rule of reason. Necessary = proportionate so, for example, the ban in *Cassis* was not proportionate, as labelling would have been enough to protect the health of consumers, but the restriction in *Cinétheque* was proportionate. This was a recognition that the rules did not have to be identical in each Member State, and that national differences, where proportionate, should be respected.

✎ **EXAM TIP**

> Because the rule of reason does not provide an exhaustive list of examples of measures which would be allowed, the rule itself and the cases that followed it can only give examples of what has been permitted in the past. Therefore if you are faced with a problem question on this subject, the scenario could also be one which falls under the rule – but it is up to you to argue the case that it is proportionate if there is no similar case to cite in example.

The second *Cassis* rule: mutual recognition

Under the second rule in *Cassis*, provided the products have been lawfully introduced into one Member State, then there should be no reason why they should not be imported into another. For example:

Case	Example
Case 16/83 *Criminal Proceedings Against Prantl* [1984] ECR 1299	Import of Italian wine into Germany in bottles whose shape was normally restricted. This was allowed because the wine was legally marketed in Italy
Case 261/81 *Walter Rau Lebensmittelwerke* v *De Smedt PVBA* [1982] ECR 3961	Belgian law restricting margarine to cube-shaped tubs prohibited because margarine was lawfully sold in other types of packaging elsewhere in the EU
Case 178/84 *Commission* v *Germany (Beer Purity Laws)* [1987] ECR 1227	Beer from other EU States that did not comply with the German beer purity law could be imported and could be called beer because it was lawfully sold in other EU States

 Make your answer stand out

The decision in *Cassis de Dijon* highlighted an important issue concerning Article 34 – that the judgment in *Dassonville* was far too broad in its scope, and therefore there were some indistinctly applicable measures which should be excused despite being breaches of Article 34 under the *Dassonville* formula. You can therefore use this point to show how the law has developed from the very simplistic position presented by the *Dassonville* formula to a more sophisticated understanding of how free movement of goods laws should be applied in the Union, with exceptions to the general rule being developed through the rule of reason. A key part of this is the fact that some of the exceptions under the rule of reason have developed from other cases that followed *Cassis*. Therefore a good knowledge of the range of cases decided under the rule of reason is an advantage when tackling a question which deals with this area of law.

See Gormley (1981) and Weiler (1999).

The liberalisation of Article 34 and indistinctly applicable measures

KEY CASE

Cases C-267 & C-268/91 *Keck & Mithouard* [1993] ECR 1–6097

Concerning: indistinctly applicable measures under Article 34 (at that time Art. 28)

Facts

A French law prohibited the resale of goods that had not been altered or repackaged at a price lower than the price at which they had been bought, in order to prevent so-called 'predatory pricing' (the process of making a short-term loss in order to force competition out of the market).

The measure was challenged as being contrary to Article 34, and the ECJ (now CJEU) modified its approach to indistinctly applicable measures on the grounds that traders had increasingly used these laws to challenge limits to their commercial freedom.

Legal principle

Where a measure was indistinctly applicable, if that measure constituted a 'selling arrangement', then it would not breach Article 34.

The phrase 'selling arrangement' has not been clearly defined. There are, however, cases which have distinguished between selling arrangements and other product-related requirements, with the latter falling outside the principle in *Keck*.

Selling arrangements	Other product-related requirements to be met
Case C-292/92 *Hünermund*: prohibition on pharmacies advertising certain pharmaceutical products outside their premises	Case C-470/93 *Vereingegen Unwesen in Handel* v *Mars*: prohibition on certain advertising claims on packaging
Case C-412/93 *Leclerc-Siplec*: prohibition on television advertising for certain products	Case C-366/04 *Schwarz*: requirement to individually package chewing gum dispensed by a vending machine

Make your answer stand out

The *Keck* case at first glance appears to be doing nothing more than splitting indistinctly applicable measures into two further sub-groups; however, the case was significant in that it halted the advanced use of Article 34 by traders where they were challenging national rules only because they limited their commercial freedom. For example, see the Sunday trading cases where DIY retailers were using European law to directly challenge the Sunday trading rules in the UK:

- Case C-145/88 *Torfaen Borough Council* v *B & Q Plc* [1989] ECR 3851.
- Case C-169/91 *Stoke-on-Trent City Council* v *B & Q Plc* [1992] ECR I-6635.
- *Wellingborough Borough Council* v *Payless DIY Ltd* [1990] 1 CMLR 773.

Keck was therefore further refining the rules concerning national differences and creating a situation whereby such differences were not to be removed just because the rules in one country were stricter than in others. This then ties in with the need for a proportionate approach – remember that the free movement of goods principles are not there to eradicate national difference just for the sake of it, and because of the *Keck* judgment, it is clear that the law now makes allowances where those differences are justified. So if you are faced with this issue in a problem question, you can ensure that you are applying the law correctly, and going beyond the *Dassonville* judgment. If you are dealing with an essay, then the finer application of free movement law presented by *Keck* can allow you to demonstrate your understanding of the evolution of EU law.

See Chalmers (1994) and Gormley (1994).

✎ EXAM TIP

The three cases of *Dassonville*, *Cassis de Dijon* and *Keck & Mithouard* form the basis of the development of the law in the area of Article 34. It is therefore essential that these cases form part of your revision on this topic – not only will they help you to understand how this area has evolved, but it will also demonstrate to the examiner that you have an understanding of how Article 34 has been applied to the cases. The rest of the case law should also form part of your revision, but you will find it more straightforward if you use these three cases as your starting point. However, remember that the law has developed beyond these three key cases, and so it is important to develop a working knowledge of more than just these cases for an effective answer to assessment questions.

■ Article 35 TFEU: restrictions on exports

KEY STATUTE

Article 35 TFEU

Quantitative restrictions on exports, and all measures having equivalent effect, shall be prohibited between Member States.

Unlike Article 34 (see Figure 7.1), there are no indistinctly applicable measures, and the *Dassonville* test does not apply. A measure has to have as its specific object the restriction

Figure 7.1

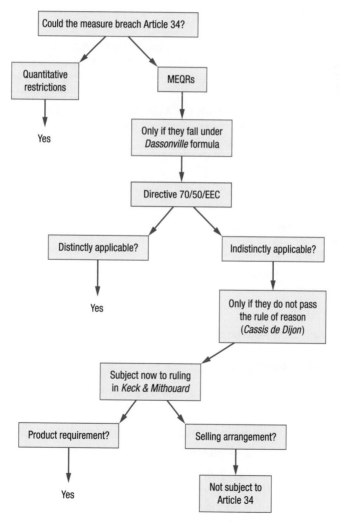

of intra-Community trade (that is, trade between Member States), and therefore it is a lot more difficult to argue this than with Article 34. Only measures which can be shown to be protectionist will breach Article 35.

Article 36 TFEU: derogations from Articles 34 and 35

KEY STATUTE

Article 36 TFEU

The provisions of Articles 34 and 35 shall not preclude prohibitions or restrictions on imports, exports or goods in transit justified on grounds of public morality, public policy or public security; the protection of health and life of humans, animals or plants; the protection of national treasures possessing artistic, historical or archaeological value; or the protection of industrial and commercial property. Such prohibitions or restrictions shall not, however, constitute a means of arbitrary discrimination or a disguised restriction on trade between Member States.

Article 36 provides situations where Member States may be excused something which is a restriction of Article 34 or 35. However:

- the list in Article 36 is *exhaustive*;
- proven ulterior motives can prevent a restriction being justified under Article 36;
- where rules have been harmonised at EU level, then a measure may not be justified under Article 36;
- provisions are narrowly construed and must satisfy the test of proportionality.

Examples of each of the areas on the list are as follows:

Article 36 justification	Case
Public morality	Compare *R* v *Henn & Darby* [1978] 1 WLR 1031 (justified prohibition on pornography due to illegality in the UK) with:
	Case 121/85 *Conegate* v *Customs & Excise* [1986] ECR 1007 (prohibition not justified as products were not prohibited in UK)
Public policy	Case 7/78 *R* v *Thompson* [1978] ECR 2247 (restriction on export of collector's coins justified because of the need to protect mint coinage)

Article 36 justification	Case
Public security	Case 72/83 *Campus Oil Ltd* [1984] ECR 2727 (requirement for importers of petroleum to buy 35 per cent of their products from the nationalised refinery allowed Ireland to maintain the ability to refine petroleum, an important security consideration)
Protection of life or health of humans, animals and plants	Case 4/75 *Rewe-Zentralfinanz GmbH* v *Landwirtschaftskammer* [1975] ECR 843 (inspection requirement which only applied to imported apples was justified because of the real risk to health from something which was not present in domestic apples)
Protection of national treasures possessing artistic, historical or archaeological value	Case 7/68 *Re Export Tax on Art Treasures* [1968] ECR 423 (quantitative restriction on export of art treasures was justified, but a tax was not)
Protection of industrial and commercial property	Case 78/70 *Deutsche Grammophon Gesellschaft mbH* v *Metro-SB-Grossmarkte GmbH* [1971] ECR 487

■ Putting it all together

Answer guidelines

See the essay question at the start of the chapter. A diagram illustrating how to structure your answer is available on the companion website.

Approaching the question

This question asks you specifically to examine the *Cassis de Dijon* case, but within the context of the law on free movement of goods, and including a discussion of how the law has developed since then. Just because the *Cassis* case is the one mentioned does not mean that this is the only case law that needs to be discussed – this question would allow you to demonstrate your understanding of the area as a whole, through a discussion of this case's place in it. You should therefore be prepared to analyse cases both before and after this judgment. Think about how you can discuss this case and its place in the development of EU law in this area. The *Dassonville* judgment is ▶

significant here, as is that of *Keck & Mithouard* mentioned in this chapter. Think about how you might tell the story of the law's development through these cases.

Important points to include

An approach to this question could include the following points:

- An introduction summarising the area of law and pointing out the important issues to be discussed in your answer; in this case, it will be centred on Article 34.
- The definition of MEQR as shown in the *Dassonville* judgment.
- A discussion of the issues raised by the inclusion of indistinctly applicable and distinctly applicable measures under Article 34.
- An assessment of the importance of the *Cassis* case, including a discussion of:
  - □ the decision made in the case itself;
  - □ the issues raised by that decision which are of more general application;
  - □ the significance of the rule of reason to the development of this area of law.
- An evaluation of how that decision may have changed the law in the area, and the significance of that change.
- The cases which have followed on from *Cassis*, and how they may have changed the application of *Cassis* and the rule of reason in EU law today, in particular the *Keck* judgment.
- A conclusion which summarises the issues and the relevance of the rule of reason to current application of EU law.

✓ Make your answer stand out

Where you are asked to answer an essay question where a specific case is mentioned in the title, there is often the temptation to write everything and anything you know about that case without thought as to structure or as to how that is going to answer the question. It is important that an answer to a question of this type has a clear logic, and that you see through the case to the context in which it sits, and are able to use the case to critically evaluate the area of law in question. Being able to produce a meaningful discussion using the case and related cases will make your answer stand out.

READ TO IMPRESS

Chalmers, D. (1994) 'Repackaging the Internal Market – the Ramifications of the *Keck* Judgment', 19 EL Rev 385

Gormley, L.W. (1981) '*Cassis de Dijon* and the Communication from the Commission', 6 EL Rev 454

Gormley, L.W. (1994) 'Reasoning Renounced? The Remarkable Judgment in *Keck and Mithouard*', EBLR 63

Steiner, J. (1992) 'Drawing the Line: Uses and Abuses of Article 30 EEC', 29 CML Rev 749

Weatherill, S. (1996) 'After *Keck*: Some Thoughts on How to Clarify the Clarification', 33 CML Rev 885

Weiler, J.J. (1999) 'From *Dassonville* to *Keck* and Beyond: An Evolutionary Reflection on the Text and Context of the Free Movement of Goods', in P. Craig and G. de Burca (eds) *The Evolution of EU Law* (Oxford University Press, Oxford), Chapter 10

www.pearsoned.co.uk/lawexpress

 Go online to access more revision support including quizzes to test your knowledge, sample questions with answer guidelines, podcasts you can download, and more!

Free movement of persons

8

Revision checklist

Essential points you should know:

☐ The general concept of EU citizenship and its importance to the European Union

☐ The basis and purpose of free movement of persons, in particular the free movement of workers and their families within the EU

☐ The rules concerning the right of an EU citizen to move freely within the EU for work

☐ Any restrictions upon that freedom of movement and their purpose

☐ Rules covering the freedom of movement of family or dependants of a worker

■ Topic map

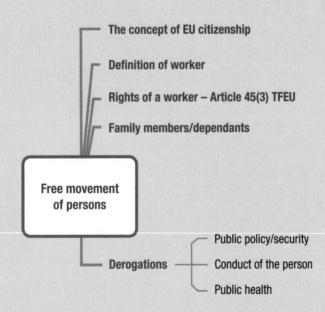

- The concept of EU citizenship
- Definition of worker
- Rights of a worker – Article 45(3) TFEU
- Family members/dependants

Free movement of persons

- Derogations
  - Public policy/security
  - Conduct of the person
  - Public health

A printable version of this topic map is available from **www.pearsoned.co.uk/lawexpress**

■ Introduction

Free movement of persons is one of the fundamental freedoms of the European Union.

It was originally established as free movement of workers, and was intended to complement the other freedoms (goods, capital, services) and therefore promote economic activity within the Community (now Union), but has now grown beyond this, and can also be seen as an important right for individuals who are EU citizens, to allow them and their families to move freely throughout the Union without restrictions. Through Directive 2004/38, the concept has been transformed into a more general one of citizenship, which works through consideration of other freedoms alongside merely the freedom to move for work. However, economic activity of persons moving around the EU remains one of the most important aspects here. This chapter reviews the rules generally concerning freedom of movement of persons, and also focuses specifically upon those classed as workers.

This chapter also reviews the related concepts of free movement of services and freedom of establishment. Some of the secondary legislation does not distinguish between employed persons and self-employed persons (who are dealt with through the rules concerning 'establishment'). These rules form the area that concerns free movement of persons generally. We will also be examining the situations in which a person may bring their family or dependants along when migrating between Member States, and any restrictions that the Member States are allowed to impose upon individuals attempting to move between Member States for work.

Where this area is assessed, it can appear in exam questions as a discrete subject of itself, but, as with most EU law, can also overlap into other areas. It is not a complex area of EU law, and you can get a good grasp of the principles through an appreciation of how the law applies to everyday life in the EU.

ASSESSMENT ADVICE

Questions in this area generally take the form of scenario-based problem questions. A question will usually involve a situation covering a person and their family either working or attempting to work in a Member State other than their own, and the application of the rules to their situation. It is most important to be familiar with the concept of 'worker' under the Treaty and relevant secondary legislation, along with the derogations and how they may be applied to the worker. Some situations can cover those who appear to be working, but do not fit within the general definition ▶

of 'worker', and therefore rules regarding the self-employed may need to be considered as well. The status of family members may also be raised as an issue in a problem question, so it is important to know the rules concerning which family members are also entitled to residence as dependants of the EU citizen, regardless of whether they are also EU citizens or not, because non-EU family members can also have rights.

■ Sample question

Could you answer this question? Below is a typical problem question that could arise on this topic. Guidelines on answering the question are included at the end of this chapter, whilst a sample essay question and guidance on tackling it can be found on the companion website.

PROBLEM QUESTION

Stefan, a Danish national, and Juanita, a Portuguese national, have been living together for three years in Denmark. They decide to try and work in the UK, and move to Manchester for this purpose.

After trying to find work for three months without success, Juanita gives up and decides to enrol at the local college in order to study fashion design. Her application for financial assistance is refused as she is not a national of the country. She invites her Brazilian grandmother, Tatiana, to stay with them in Manchester, but on her arrival in the UK, Tatiana is refused entry.

Stefan, in the meantime, has found part-time work as a parcel courier, but Juanita is asked to leave the country, as she and Stefan are not married. Further, Stefan's employer is suspected of using his business to cover a drug smuggling ring and, as a result, Stefan is rounded up by the police and recommended for deportation as 'undesirable'.

Advise Stefan, Juanita and Tatiana of their rights in EU law.

■ The concept of EU citizenship

The overarching principle which affects all aspects of freedom for persons is that of EU citizenship. This is now enshrined in the TFEU, as follows:

KEY STATUTE

Article 20(1) TFEU

Every person holding the nationality of a Member State shall be a citizen of the Union.

There are several fundamental rights associated with this, they are:

- free movement;
- voting;
- diplomatic protection;
- petitioning of the European Ombudsman.

! Don't be tempted to . . .

. . . think of EU citizenship as being like citizenship of a country. Although this concept was introduced to develop a sense of belonging to citizens of EU Member States, the right itself is not absolute, as shown in the two cases below.

KEY CASE

R v *Secretary of State for the Home Department, ex parte Vitale and Do Amaral* [1996] 2 CMLR 587

Concerning: the scope of EU citizenship

Facts

This case concerned two EU citizens who had been living in the UK for some time, claiming income support from the UK government. They had not got jobs, and showed no signs of getting one – they seemed quite content to live on the benefits they were receiving and had no other form of income.

The UK government decided that, as they were not seeking work, they should be required to leave, and attempted to get them to do so. Vitale and Do Amaral argued that they had a general right to remain as EU citizens, and therefore irrespective of whether they found work or not, they could not be required to leave.

Legal principle

The judge in this case pointed out that neither the right to move freely nor the right to reside were absolute and were subject to the limitations of the Treaties. Vitale and Do Amaral therefore did not have an absolute right to live in the UK and could be required to leave.

KEY CASE

Case C-299/95 *Kremzow* v *Austria* [1997] ECR I-2629

Concerning: the concept of EU citizenship

Facts

This case involved a person attempting to use the fact of their EU citizenship to argue that he should be protected by EU law with regard to criminal proceedings brought against him.

Legal principle

Again, the Court refused to give an all-encompassing right to a citizen under this right – it has to be subject to the limitations of the Treaties, and is not a blanket right, but is there for specific purposes. In the same way that EU law does not cover every aspect of life within each Member State, citizenship is not a blanket concept.

Other rights associated with citizenship

There are other rights which are an important part of citizenship of the EU, mainly because they can be used in a tangible way in other parts of the free movement of persons principle. These are set out below.

Article 18 TFEU – Non-discrimination on grounds of nationality

Article 18 prohibits discrimination against an EU citizen on grounds of nationality. This has allowed the ECJ to combine the two concepts of citizenship and non-discrimination in the following case, which elevates citizenship somewhat.

KEY CASE

Case C-184/99 *Grzelczyk* v *Centre Public d'aide sociale d'Ottignies-Louvain-la-Neuve* [2001] ECR I-6193

Concerning: non-discrimination under Article 18 TFEU

Facts

This case involved a French student who applied for a Belgian social security benefit called 'minimex', or minimum subsistence allowance. He was refused. When he took his case to a Belgian tribunal, they referred the matter on to the CJEU, who had to decide whether the rule regarding who was entitled to minimex was compatible with Article 18.

Legal principle

The Court came to the conclusion that the only thing stopping the student from getting the benefit was his nationality – a Belgian student in the same situation would have been entitled to this benefit. The Court therefore concluded that, as this was the case, the Belgian law was incompatible with Article 18. They said:

> Union citizenship is destined to be the fundamental status of nationals of the Member States, enabling those who find themselves in the same situation to enjoy the same treatment in law irrespective of their nationality, subject to such exceptions as are expressly provided for.

Article 19 TFEU: non-discrimination based on sex, racial or ethnic origin, religion or belief, disability, age or sexual orientation

Similarly, Article 19 prohibits discrimination on a wide range of grounds. This Article has led to specific Directives on these issues: for example, Directive 2000/43/EC on racial/ethnic equality and Directive 2000/78/EC on equality in employment rights.

▓ Free movement of workers under the Treaties

The main concept associated with free movement of persons concerns the movement of workers. The concept of free movement of workers is enshrined in the Treaty as one of the four fundamental freedoms. The freedom itself is contained in Article 45 of the TFEU, along with the powers given to the EU to make secondary legislation on the matter in Article 46 TFEU.

KEY STATUTE

Article 45(1) and (2) TFEU

(1) Freedom of movement for workers shall be secured within the Community.

(2) Such freedom of movement shall entail the abolition of any discrimination based on nationality between workers of the Member States as regards employment, remuneration and other conditions of work and employment.

This Article makes three important points:

- A worker is entitled to move freely throughout the EU for the purposes of getting a job and performing that job (Art. 45(1) and (3) TFEU).
- A worker has the right not to be discriminated against based on their nationality (Art. 45(2) TFEU).
- That right is subject to several exceptions (Art. 45(2) and (4) TFEU).

This Article, however, does not contain a lot of detail concerning how this is to be put into practice (it does not even define 'worker', for example) and therefore there is a right contained in Article 46 TFEU giving the EU the right to make secondary legislation in order to provide the detail needed.

✎ EXAM TIP

Bear in mind also that the rules allowing workers to move freely around the EU also allow persons generally to do this too. You often do not have to prove you are a worker to gain entry to a Member State, and many people just moving around the EU as tourists can also take advantages of these freedoms, as you may have gathered when going through the 'Blue' channel at airport customs.

■ Free movement of workers under secondary legislation

Free movement of workers is primarily dealt with through the secondary legislation, Regulation 1612/68 and Directive 2004/38. The role of these pieces of legislation is to provide the detail that the TFEU does not provide.

■ Definition of 'worker'

When dealing with this area, the first thing you must establish is that the person concerned is classed as a **worker**. In most circumstances, this will be a fairly straightforward question, although in some cases the answer is not as obvious as appears. If we start from basic principles, a worker can be defined as follows:

KEY DEFINITION: Worker

Workers are EU nationals who are either in employment (full or part time) in that they are paid in return for their performance under an employer/employee relationship, or are seeking actual paid work.

This definition does not come from the Treaty, but can be explained by the case law surrounding this area. Article 45 failed to define what a worker was, and therefore the CJEU has taken a broad approach to defining 'worker' through the case law. Below are some examples of decisions from the CJEU on the definition of 'worker', but first, the *Lawrie-Blum* case provides a general explanation.

KEY CASE

Case 66/85 *Lawrie-Blum* v *Land Baden-Württemburg* [1986] ECR 2121

Concerning: definition of 'worker' under Article 45 TFEU

Facts

This case concerned a trainee teacher in Germany. The German government attempted to argue that Lawrie-Blum was not a 'worker' because of his trainee status.

Legal principle

The CJEU found that the trainee teacher was a 'worker', and set out a three-part test to deal with the issue. They defined a 'worker' as someone who:

(1) during a certain period of time

(2) performs services for and under the direction of another

(3) in return for remuneration.

Other case law has also taken this broad approach to defining a worker. The concept of worker has two parts: an economic part and a formal part.

Economic aspect of 'worker'

A worker has to be performing duties in exchange for some economic gain, whether that be money or otherwise. The table below gives examples of how the courts have dealt with the economic part of this.

Case	Principle
Case 53/81 *Levin* v *Staatssecretaris van Justitie* [1982] ECR 1035	The definition of worker included those doing part-time work
Case 196/87 *Steymann* v *Staatssecretaris van Justitie* [1988] ECR 6159	Payment for work did not have to be monetary, but could be a benefit in kind
Case 139/85 *Kempf* v *Staatssecretaris van Justitie* [1986] ECR 1741	Someone who does not earn enough to live on (and therefore must also claim benefits) is still a worker

Formal aspect of 'worker'

On the formal aspect, a worker must be someone defined as 'employed'. Therefore, you would expect an employer/employee relationship to exist, with the employee taking instructions from the employer.

Case	Principle
Case 66/85 *Lawrie-Blum* v *Land Baden-Württemburg* [1986] ECR 2121	Someone who performs a service under the direction of another
Case 75/63 *Hoekstra* v *BBDA* [1964] ECR 177	A worker could also be someone who had recently lost their job, and was looking to take another one
Case 139/85 *Kempf* v *Staatssecretaris van Justitie* [1986] ECR 1741	Whether an individual earns enough to live on through the work is irrelevant

✎ EXAM TIP

Remember that this definition of 'worker' excludes anyone who is self-employed. These persons are not classed as 'workers' under the Treaties. There are separate rules which deal with free movement for people providing services, and people wishing to establish themselves. This may or may not be part of the syllabus of your EU law course, but it is important to remember that they are dealt with elsewhere in the Treaty, and therefore the definition of worker is quite a restrictive one.

Working and seeking work

It is often necessary to enter a Member State in order to get work, so those looking for work are treated in a similar fashion to workers, but only for a limited time.

KEY CASE

Case C-292/89 *R* v *Immigration Appeal Tribunal, ex parte Antonissen* [1991] ECR I-745

Concerning: status as 'worker' when seeking work in another Member State

Facts

Antonissen was appealing against a decision to deport him, claiming free movement as a worker under Article 48 (then 39, now Art. 45 TFEU) as he had been looking for work in the UK. However, he had not found any for over six months.

Legal principle

The CJEU held that it was reasonable for the Member State to deport someone if they had not found work within six months.

Article 6 of Directive 2004/38 allows any EU national to remain in any Member State for up to three months without having to conform to the definition of 'worker', but beyond this, unless there is a realistic chance of them getting a job, they can be required to leave the State concerned.

✎ EXAM TIP

The simple answer to the issue of seeking work is to apply a time limit of three months, because from Directive 2004/38 it appears reasonable to come to this conclusion. However, this is a grey area, because if a person can show that they are *seeking* employment, and have a realistic chance of getting a job, then they may be able to show they have a right to stay, even though the three-month period has expired. Deeper thinking like this will enable you to show a better understanding of the subject when tackling an exam question. The point about the time limit was emphasised in Case C-138/02 *Brian Francis Collins* v *Secretary of State for Work and Pensions* [2004] ECR I-2703, so in theory a person could stay in a Member State a lot longer, although the Member State is allowed to lay down a reasonable time limit.

■ Rights of a worker

KEY STATUTE

Article 45(3) TFEU

3 It shall entail the right, subject to limitations justified on grounds of public policy, public security or public health:

(a) to accept offers of employment actually made;

(b) to move freely within the territory of Member States for this purpose;

(c) to stay in a Member State for the purpose of employment in accordance with the provisions governing the employment of nationals of that State laid down by law, regulation or administrative action;

(d) to remain in the territory of a Member State after having been employed in that State, subject to conditions which shall be embodied in implementing regulations to be drawn up by the Commission.

The rights outlined above are dealt with generally by Directive 2004/38. All rights concerning movement into or out of a Member State are subject to the need to have a valid passport. In summary, the most important of these rights are:

Right	Source
Right to enter	Article 5(1) Directive 2004/38
Right to leave	Article 4(1) Directive 2004/38
Right to reside	■ Without a job (up to three months): Article 6 Directive 2004/38 ■ With a job: Article 7 Directive 2004/38
Right to remain after losing a job	Article 7(3) Directive 2004/38, if: ■ temporarily unable to work because of illness ■ involuntarily unemployed and seeking work ■ started vocational training
Right of permanent residence	Article 16(1) Directive 2004/38 after continuous residence of five years

It should also be noted that the rights of entry and exit, residence, ability to bring family members and also remain after (self) employment also apply to those exercising rights under establishment and services.

Public sector work

Jobs in the public sector are specifically excluded under Article 45(4) TFEU. It is important for the government of a country to restrict certain public sector jobs to their own nationals.

Non-discrimination under Article 45(2) TFEU

KEY STATUTE

Article 45(2) TFEU

Such freedom of movement shall entail the abolition of any discrimination based on nationality between workers of the Member States as regards employment, remuneration and other conditions of work and employment.

Regulation 1612/68 outlaws many obstacles to migrant workers in its first 12 Articles. This therefore means that a worker is allowed access to the same jobs, tax and social advantages as if they were a national of that country. However, Member States are justified in withholding social assistance (including financial) during the first three months of the worker's residence (see Art. 24(2) of Directive 2004/38). They can also withhold any financial support for training or studying until the worker has permanent residence rights.

▇ Freedom of establishment and freedom to provide services

There are circumstances in which an individual may have free movement, but in a situation which is not covered in the rather focused definition of 'worker'. This centres on the other freedoms we are going to cover here, those of freedom of establishment, and freedom to provide services. There are specific rules regarding these within the Treaties.

Freedom of establishment

The right of establishment is another key aspect of the free movement rights in the EU. This right gives EU citizens and their families the right to move and establish themselves in other EU Member States.

KEY STATUTE

Article 49 TFEU

Within the framework of the provisions set out below, restrictions on the freedom of establishment of nationals of a Member State in the territory of another Member State shall be prohibited. Such prohibition shall also apply to restrictions on the setting-up of agencies, branches or subsidiaries by nationals of any Member State established in the territory of any Member State.

Freedom of establishment shall include the right to take up and pursue activities as self-employed persons and to set up and manage undertakings, in particular companies or firms within the meaning of the second paragraph of Article 54, under the conditions laid down for its own nationals by the law of the country where such establishment is effected, subject to the provisions of the Chapter relating to capital.

The freedom to move generally between Member States has long been accepted, and therefore the main barrier to freedom of establishment has not been the ability to travel physically to other Member States, but the recognition of qualifications once attempting to establish there.

Directive 2005/36/EC

The system of recognition of professional qualifications used to be regulated by a number of different Directives on different subjects. However, this is now all covered by Directive 2005/36/EC, which deals with those who temporarily offer services in a Member State, as well as those who permanently establish themselves there.

Professional qualifications are those relating to 'regulated professions' (in other words, those with a professional governing body that regulates practice in that field), and the Directive established a system of mutual recognition of qualifications between the Member States.

Some professions are automatically recognised, and therefore do not have to be individually assessed:

- Doctors
- Nurses
- Dentists
- Veterinarians
- Midwives
- Pharmacists
- Architects.

However, for the remainder, the qualification of a person to carry out a profession is assessed based upon level of qualifications, as well as years of professional experience where appropriate.

Non-professional qualifications

Other qualifications not covered by Directive 2005/36/EC are assessed by the courts based upon the requirements of Article 49.

KEY CASE

Case 222/86 *UNECTEF* v *Heylens* [1987] ECR 4097
Concerning: assessment of non-professional qualifications

Facts

Heylens was a Belgian who had a diploma in football training from Belgium. He moved to France to train with the French national team, but when he applied for recognition of his diploma, it was refused. He continued to work with the football team, and was prosecuted by the French football trainers' union.

Legal principle

In deciding his case, the CJEU decided that Heylens' diploma must be assessed against 'the level of knowledge and qualifications which its holder can be assumed to possess in the light of that diploma' having regard to 'the nature and duration of the studies and practical training which the diploma certifies that he has carried out'.

Freedom to provide services

Alongside the freedom of establishment is the freedom to provide services. A service provider is defined in the TFEU as follows:

KEY STATUTE

Article 57 TFEU

Services shall be considered to be 'services' within the meaning of the Treaties where they are normally provided for remuneration, in so far as they are not governed by the provisions relating to freedom of movement for goods, capital and persons.

Services are defined as an economic activity but, beyond that, are more defined by what they are *not*, rather than what they are. The definition excludes anything which may be covered by one of the other freedoms. The situation with regard to freedom to provide services is now covered by the Services Directive 2006/123:

KEY STATUTE

Directive 2006/123, Article 16

Member States shall respect the right of providers to provide services in a Member State other than that in which they are established.

The Member State in which the service is provided shall ensure free access to and free exercise of a service activity within its territory.

Article 16 goes on to lay down examples of actions that Member States are prohibited from taking as they may hinder the freedom to provide services, and also provides derogations similar to those for workers. We will deal with these later in this chapter.

Rights to receive services

Although the TFEU makes no mention of those who wish to receive services, this is also dealt with, by case law, for example:

Case	Receipt of services
Case 286/82 and 26/83 *Luisi and Carbone* v *Ministero del Tesoro* [1984] ECR 377	Italian attempts to prevent persons taking large amounts of currency out of Italy were contrary to the freedom to receive services because the money was to pay for those services ▶

Case	Receipt of services
Case 45/93 *Commission* v *Spain* [1994] ECR I-911	Spanish authorities were not permitted to charge citizens of other EU countries entry to museums where Spanish citizens were not charged as this interfered with other EU nationals' freedom to receive tourism services
Case C-158/96 *Kohll* v *Union des Caisses de Maladie* [1998] ECR I-1931	Healthcare was considered to be a 'service' and therefore EU citizens had a right to receive such a service in another Member State (subject to different rules in different states regarding funding of that treatment)

■ Rights of family members and dependants of workers

When a person moves within the Single Market, of course their family and dependants will need to move as well. The Treaty does not mention family members. However, Article 2(2) of Directive 2004/38 gives details of family members and dependants who have the right to move into the Member State with a worker (Figure 8.1). Most of these rules also apply to those who are moving to another Member State to establish themselves.

! Don't be tempted to . . .

When considering descendants and dependants under 21, it is important to note that children of either the worker or their spouse have particularly special status: the term 'children' includes all children of either partner, not just those who are common to both the worker and their partner. They also remain part of the worker's family, even after a divorce has taken place. They are also protected by Article 8 of the European Convention on Human Rights, which protects the right to family life. Article 12 of Directive 2004/38 also gives them the same right to education as nationals of that State. Consider carefully the rights of these dependants, and make sure you are aware of how the rules apply to them.

Figure 8.1

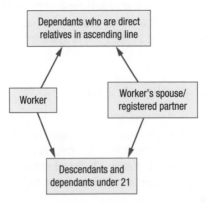

 Make your answer stand out

The situation concerning family members can become complicated – because where the situation involves a worker, their status will be dependent upon the status of the worker, and in this way they can be disadvantaged. You must therefore think carefully about their status, and deal with the status of the worker first before dealing with the dependant. This will prevent you contradicting yourself in your answer, particularly if that issue is in the exam. Also bear in mind that rules regarding workers' families do not always cover those exercising other freedoms.

See Woods (1999).

■ Derogations from free movement of workers, establishment and services

KEY DEFINITION: Derogation

The exemption from, or the relaxation of, a particular law. In this context, exceptions to the rule requiring free movement.

The right of free movement is not absolute – you also have to bear in mind that there are some circumstances in which a Member State can either refuse entry to an individual, or require them to leave. In relation to workers, if you look at Article 45(3), it refers to the rights of a worker being generally 'subject to limitations justified on grounds of public policy, public security or public health'. Similar **derogations** are contained in Article 16 of Directive 2006/123 with regard to services. The phrase used is quite vague, and Directive 2004/38 deals with specifics of how it is to be applied. It is possible to see its influence in refining these quite general concepts.

Public policy and public security

The public policy ground for excluding migrant workers is probably the vaguest of the three derogations, and therefore potentially most open to abuse by a Member State that wants to justify excluding someone. Public security is also generally considered at the same time, as the two concepts overlap. The ECJ's (now CJEU's) approach has been to give the public policy ground for exclusion a very narrow meaning. Have a look at the evolution of this concept in the table below.

Case/Article	Meaning of 'public policy'
Case 41/74 *van Duyn* v *Home Office* [1974] ECR 1337	Activities/membership of an organisation considered to be 'socially harmful'
Case 30/77 *R* v *Bouchereau* [1977] ECR 1999	Activities which are a genuine and sufficiently serious threat to the requirements of public policy affecting one of the fundamental interests of society
Article 27(2) Directive 2004/38	'Must represent a genuine, present and sufficiently serious threat affecting one of the fundamental interests of society'

There are also several other considerations under Directive 2004/38. Member States are not allowed to use the public policy derogation in the following circumstances:

Article of Directive 2004/38	Exception
Article 15(2)	Not having a passport or ID card is not grounds for expelling a person
Article 27(1)	Prohibits excluding a person for economic purposes
Article 27(2)	Previous criminal convictions on their own are not enough to exclude a person if this of itself is not indicative of the citizen's possible current threat to the State

Conduct of the person

A reason for excluding someone under public policy or public security has to be based on the conduct or behaviour of the person concerned – see Article 27(2) of Directive 2004/38. The important factor to remember is that the behaviour or activity of that person must be current, and not merely something in that person's past. The following are some key case examples.

KEY CASE

Case 41/74 *Van Duyn* v *Home Office* [1974] ECR 1337

Concerning: exclusion of a migrant worker on grounds of public policy based upon association with a particular group

Facts

Van Duyn was a Dutch woman who wanted to enter the UK to take up a job working within the Church of Scientology in the UK. Although not a banned organisation, it was viewed by the UK government as undesirable. The Home Office refused her entry on grounds that her conduct, as a member of this organisation, was contrary to public policy.

Legal principle

The ECJ (now CJEU) decided that the concept of public policy had to be interpreted narrowly, but that a Member State had a certain amount of discretion as to how it was to be applied. Therefore van Duyn's *current* membership of this organisation could constitute grounds for refusing her entry, even where it was not a banned organisation. The activity has to be considered 'socially harmful'.

KEY CASE

Case 30/77 *R* v *Bouchereau* [1977] ECR 1999

Concerning: criminal convictions as 'conduct' under public policy grounds for exclusion

Facts

Mr Bouchereau was a Frenchman who had been convicted on several occasions of drug possession. Because of his convictions, the UK were attempting to expel him, and claimed they were justified in doing so because of his conduct.

Legal principle

The activities of the person concerned must be socially harmful in order to justify expelling him.

✎ EXAM TIP

The important point of the above case is that it's not just a history of criminal convictions that allows a person to be expelled – the longer the time since the conviction, the less likely it is to be relevant. Therefore, it is important to weigh up the seriousness of the criminal offence and how long ago it was committed if faced with a scenario that includes a person with a criminal record.

KEY CASE

Case 67/74 *Bonsignore* v *Oberstadtdirektor of the City of Cologne* **[1975] ECR 297**
Concerning: expulsion under public security used preventatively

Facts

Bonsignore was an Italian working in Germany. He was convicted of a minor firearms offence and the German government attempted to deport him back to Italy. They claimed it was in order to deter other immigrants from committing similar offences.

Legal principle

The argument was rejected. The ECJ (now CJEU) said that the reason had to be about the possible future behaviour of that person, not in order generally to prevent others from following his example.

Public health

This has a broader scope than the other two derogations. According to Article 29 of Directive 2004/38, it is limited to the following:

- 'Diseases with epidemic potential'.
- 'Other infectious diseases or contagious parasitic diseases'.

The important thing here is that this is also limited in time (unlike the other two derogations). If a disease is contracted more than three months after the worker has entered the country, then it cannot be a reason for expelling them. Also, HIV/AIDS is excepted.

■ Putting it all together

Answer guidelines

See the problem question at the start of the chapter.

Approaching the question

This question requires you to consider the rights of three individuals, two of whom are EU nationals while the other is not. You must first consider the rights of the two EU nationals, and then any rights that the non-EU national may have in relation to them. It is important therefore to approach this question in a methodical way, dealing with one person at a time.

Important points to include

Consider:

- Stefan and Juanita are entitled to live in the UK for up to three months looking for work (Art. 6 of Directive 2004/38).

- Stefan has found a job, but it is part time; does this allow him to be classed as a worker? See *Levin*. Consider whether he falls within the definition of worker.

- Juanita has not found work; can she still be classed as a 'worker'? Consider whether she is entitled to any support in relation to her education under Directive 2004/38 either as a worker, or as part of Stefan's 'family'. Also, consider whether she is entitled to remain in the country either as a 'worker' or as part of Stefan's 'family'. Can she say she is actively seeking work?

- Tatiana is not an EU national, and therefore does not have any rights of free movement as a worker, but is she part of the family of a worker? See Article 2(2) of Directive 2004/38.

- Can Stefan be deported merely for his association with a suspected drug trafficker? Look at public policy grounds for derogation from free movement of workers under Article 45(2).

- This question has focused upon the provisions regarding workers, but you should also consider whether a scenario in a problem question like this is affected by establishment and services rules as well.

▶

Make your answer stand out

You must consider the way in which the ECJ (now CJEU) has approached the application of these rules, and not just the rules themselves. A good answer to this question will consider the broad or narrow interpretation placed upon the rights and exceptions in this area in order to provide an accurate application of the law to the facts, which should result in clear advice to the parties concerned. Don't just reiterate facts – remember this is about advising the parties concerned, so you will need to show you understand the rules *and* how they apply.

READ TO IMPRESS

Castro Oliveira, A. (2002) 'Workers and Other Persons: Step-by-step from Movement to Citizenship', 39 CML Rev 77

Cygan, A. (2013) 'Citizenship of the European Union', 62 ICLQ 492

Dougan, M. (2005) 'Fees, Grants, Loans and Dole Cheques: Who Covers the Cost of Migrant Education within the EU?', 42 CML Rev 943

Woods, L. (1999) 'Family Rights in the EU – Disadvantaging the Disadvantaged?', 11 *Child & Family Law Quarterly* 17

www.pearsoned.co.uk/lawexpress

 Go online to access more revision support including quizzes to test your knowledge, sample questions with answer guidelines, podcasts you can download, and more!

Competition law

9

Revision checklist

Essential points you should know:

- [ ] The purpose behind the use of Articles 101 and 102 to regulate competition law in Europe
- [ ] The definitions applied in the Treaty to both Articles 101 and 102
- [ ] The way in which Article 101 is applied to anti-competitive agreements
- [ ] The application of exemptions to Article 101, such as block exemptions and comfort letters
- [ ] The application of Article 102 to anti-competitive abuses of a dominant position

■ Topic map

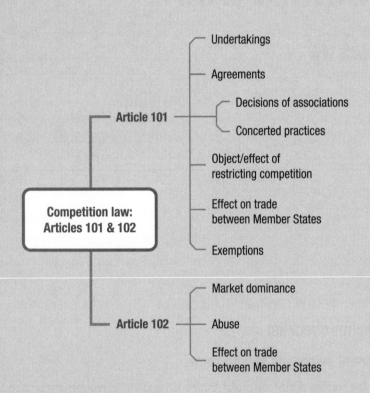

Competition law: Articles 101 & 102

Article 101
- Undertakings
- Agreements
  - Decisions of associations
  - Concerted practices
- Object/effect of restricting competition
- Effect on trade between Member States
- Exemptions

Article 102
- Market dominance
- Abuse
- Effect on trade between Member States

■ Introduction

Competition law in Articles 101 and 102 TFEU is just one aspect of the rules set up by the EU to regulate the Single Market.

The aim is to ensure that there is as free a market as possible, but with enough regulation to ensure that the market is not abused. Articles 101 and 102 are therefore only a part of this, but a key part. These two Treaty Articles prohibit:

- Anti-competitive agreements between **undertakings** and restrictive practices
- Abuse by a company of a dominant position in the market.

When looking at these rules, it is important to note the context within which they sit: they are part of the measures aimed at the smooth running of the Single European Market, and you should also bear in mind that there are rules for Member States to follow (regarding free movement and the customs union) and also anti-dumping measures, and so although an examination question may not cover all these areas, you should always remember that Articles 101 and 102 exist in this wider context.

This chapter examines the rules in Articles 101 and 102, and looks at how they have been applied in practice through the case law. This should therefore allow you to consider the use of these rules in a practical context (useful for problem questions) and also their more theoretical aspects (useful for essay questions).

ASSESSMENT ADVICE

Questions on this area of law can vary according to the way in which competition law is taught at your university, as the focus of the subject can vary greatly. However, they tend to rely heavily upon the case law, as the development of this area has tended to take place incrementally through the cases.

Problem questions

Are probably the most straightforward to deal with, as they will be looking for the application of the law to the scenario outlined in the question. As EU competition law is heavily based on the criteria in Articles 101 and 102, this can be a fairly straightforward exercise if you are also prepared to discuss a range of cases that help to illustrate the application of these principles.

Essay questions

Will also call for knowledge of the cases, as the question will require knowledge of this area beyond the rules and definitions in the Treaty.

■ Sample question

Could you answer this question? Below is a typical essay question that could arise on this topic. Guidelines on answering the question are included at the end of this chapter, whilst a sample problem question and guidance on tackling it can be found on the companion website.

ESSAY QUESTION

Critically evaluate the effect of the introduction of Regulation 1/2003 on Article 101. Does the system under this Regulation have any advantages beyond merely reducing the workload of the Commission in granting individual exemptions?

■ Article 101 TFEU: anti-competitive agreements between undertakings

KEY STATUTE

Article 101(1) and (2) TFEU

(1) The following shall be prohibited as incompatible with the common market: all agreements between undertakings, decisions by associations of undertakings and concerted practices which may affect trade between Member States and which have as their object or effect the prevention, restriction or distortion of competition within the common market, and in particular those which:

   (a) directly or indirectly fix purchase or selling prices or any other trading conditions;

   (b) limit or control production, markets, technical development, or investment;

   (c) share markets or sources of supply;

   (d) apply dissimilar conditions to equivalent transactions with other trading parties, thereby placing them at a competitive disadvantage;

   (e) make the conclusion of contracts subject to acceptance by the other parties of supplementary obligations which, by their nature or according to commercial usage, have no connection with the subject of such contracts.

(2) Any agreements or decisions prohibited pursuant to this Article shall be automatically void.

Figure 9.1

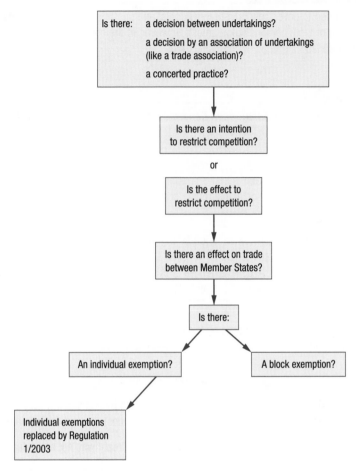

Article 101's purpose is to prevent any restrictive practices which may have an effect on competition in the EU (Figure 9.1). It is very specific about the type of activities it includes (those listed under (a) to (e) in the extract from Art. 101 above), although this list is not exhaustive. In order to understand Article 101, you need to break it down into its different parts.

To whom does Article 101 apply?

Article 101 is aimed at private bodies, or '**undertakings**' as it says in the Treaty. It is *not* there to deal with the activities of governments or the public sector – they are dealt with by other parts of the Treaty.

KEY DEFINITION: Undertakings

This is intended to cover only private individuals, and so it means natural persons (such as you and I) or legal persons (companies). However, in the context of Article 101, it has also been defined as groups of companies too.

KEY CASE

Case C-159/91 *Pucet* v *Assurances Générales de France* [1993] ECR I-637

Concerning: definition of 'undertaking'

Facts

This case concerned accusations that a regional social security organisation had been anti-competitive regarding social insurance 'services'.

Legal principle

In deciding whether a body was an 'undertaking', the Court of Justice decided that there was a distinction to be made based on whether the body concerned was engaged in economic activities as such, or whether, as in this case, the body pursued activities on the basis of solidarity and with no intention to make a profit.

Some examples of bodies considered by the Court of Justice as to whether they are 'undertakings' under Article 101 are shown in the following table.

Case	Is it an 'undertaking'?
Case C-343/95 *Diego Cali* v *SEPG*	A body established by national law (in this case to collect harbour duties) was not an undertaking
Case C-364/92 *SAT* v *Eurocontrol*	A body set up by Treaty was not an undertaking
Case C-519/04P *Meca-Medina and Majcen* v *Commission*	A sporting body (such as the International Olympic Committee) could be an undertaking

What does Article 101 prohibit?

There are three broad categories of what the Article prohibits: 'agreements between undertakings, decisions by associations of undertakings and concerted practices'.

Activity	Meaning
Agreements between undertakings	Can be both binding/non-binding, written or verbal. Can even include 'gentlemen's agreements'

Activity	Meaning
Decisions by associations of undertakings	Binding or non-binding instructions/recommendations by trade associations to members
Concerted practices	Action by competitors in a market arising from them coordinating their actions, such as coordinated price rises by different companies where there is no plausible explanation other than the concerted practice

This means that Article 101 can have a broad coverage. Some examples of what can fall within the different categories follow.

Agreements

Case	Agreement
Case 32/78 *BMW Belgium* v *Commission*	Belgian car dealers signed a document agreeing to the manufacturer's request not to sell cars in other Member States
Case C-338/00 *Volkswagen* v *Commission*	A telephone call by the manufacturer to car dealers instructing them not to do something
Case IV/35.733 *Community* v *Volkswagen AG and Others*	Request to car dealers not to re-export cars (even though the car dealers' compliance was extracted by heavy pressure)

Decisions by associations of undertakings

This is where a trade association will issue a set of instructions to its members or make an agreement with its members, for example, fixing prices on products sold by its members, as this can allow dominant sellers in the market to keep their dominant position and prevent other companies from competing with them.

Concerted practices

Although in the first two examples there has to be evidence of an agreement in place, the idea of concerted practices is a lot wider, although it is still down to the Commission to get evidence to show that what is happening is a concerted practice, and not just everyone raising their prices when one company does, as happens with petrol prices. There has to be consistent evidence of a concerted practice, but that can be one of a number of things, to conclusively be considered a concerted practice. See the following key case.

KEY CASE

Cases 11, 40–48, 50, 56, 113–114/73 *Suiker Unie* v *Commission* [1975] ECR 1663
Concerning: meaning of 'concerted practice'

Facts

Sugar producers in the EU had decided only to import into Holland with permission from the main Dutch producers. Doing this meant that there was less pressure on the Dutch sugar producers to compete than there would have been had the other producers just imported into the country without their permission. They were accused of engaging in a concerted practice, but claimed they were not because there was no agreement between the different sugar producers to do this.

Legal principle

The ECJ (now CJEU) held that it was not necessary for there to be a specific understanding in order for this to be a concerted practice. It just needed to involve some sort of contact, whether it be direct or indirect, which led to the action (like price-fixing) taking place. A concerted practice allows competitors to fix a position in the knowledge of what others are going to do.

Object or effect of restricting competition

In some situations it is possible to show that there was intention to restrict competition, but, even if this is not the case, if it can be shown that the effect (whether intended or not) was to restrict competition, then this will be enough.

✎ EXAM TIP

Remember when looking at this issue that if you are dealing with a problem question, you need to look at the effect *within the relevant market*, so it is important to be able to define the relevant product market, or the relevant geographical area. A relevant market may be broad, for example 'fruit', or it may be narrow, for example 'bananas'.

There are also two types of agreement that can have an effect on the relevant market, and Article 101 applies to both of them:

Type of agreement	Definition
Vertical agreements	Between those on different levels, e.g. imposed upon a distributor by the supplier
Horizontal agreements	Between firms that operate on the same level in the market

KEY CASE

Cases 56 & 58/64 *Consten* v *Commission* **[1966] ECR 299**
Concerning: types of agreements covered by Article 101

Facts

This case concerned an agreement between a supplier and their distributor for products to be sold in France. An agreement was made between them that the distributor would not sell outside France, and in return the supplier agreed to make agreements with its other European distributors that they would not sell in France. The agreement was challenged under Article 101 when another distributor (from Germany) started selling the products in France at a lower price.

Legal principle

The ECJ (now CJEU) decided that the agreement was contrary to Article 101, and in doing so, it made several important points:

- Article 101 could apply to vertical agreements (as this one was) as well as horizontal ones.

- The fact that this agreement had streamlined and increased distribution of the product in question was irrelevant.

- The important point here was that the agreement had harmed the Single European Market by an attempt to repartition along national boundaries.

Examples of what is prohibited in Article 101(1)

The list in Article 101(1) is not meant to be exclusive – there are other things which potentially could breach Article 101 *if* they meet the criteria discussed above. However, they are a good starting point. They are as follows:

- directly or indirectly fix purchase or selling prices or any other trading conditions;

- limit or control production, markets, technical development, or investment;

- share markets or sources of supply;

- apply dissimilar conditions to equivalent transactions with other trading parties, thereby placing them at a competitive disadvantage;

- make the conclusion of contracts subject to acceptance by the other parties of supplementary obligations which, by their nature or according to commercial usage, have no connection with the subject of such contracts.

Effect on trade between Member States

> **! Don't be tempted to . . .**
>
> You must be wary of assuming that action can be taken in trivial circumstances (referred to as situations of *de minimis*). Both Articles 101 and 102 deal with activities that may affect free competition within the EU. However, not all agreements or abuses may be subject to this rule. Have a look at Case 5/69 *Volk* v *Vervaecke* [1969] ECR 295, where it was decided that the agreement didn't breach Article 101 because it didn't have a significant effect on the market. (The effect was *de minimis*.) However, in Case 23/67 *Brasserie de Haecht* v *Wilkin* [1967] ECR 407, if there are several agreements which when added together do have a significant effect, then they will breach Article 101.
>
> In order for something to satisfy this aspect of Article 101, it must either have:
>
> - a direct or indirect effect on trade between Member States, or
> - the capability of such an effect.
>
> This is a very wide definition, and is made wider still by the fact that the term 'trade' is also given a very wide meaning (although as can be seen regarding the definition of 'undertaking' mentioned earlier in this chapter, economic activity is important), but significantly, if it doesn't affect trade between Member States, then it should be dealt with by national law, and not EU law.

Exemptions from Article 101 TFEU

It is possible for an agreement under Article 101 not to be declared void if it fulfils *all* of the following conditions:

- it contributes to improving production or distribution of goods or to promoting technical or economic progress;
- it allows consumers a fair share of this benefit;
- it does not impose conditions that are not necessary to achieve the above;
- it does not allow undertakings to eliminate a substantial amount of competition.

Application of exemptions

There were previously three ways of gaining an exemption:

Method of exemption	Explanation
Individual exemption	Application to the Commission for a decision as to whether the agreement falls within Article 101(3). This has now been removed by Regulation 1/2003
Comfort letter	An alternative to the individual decision, this is an informal opinion from the Commission that the agreement does not breach Article 101. Saves time, but is non-binding and has no legal effect. Also now essentially defunct
Block exemption	Blanket exemptions in certain industries passed by regulation. Again, this saves Commission time, by allowing blanket exemption in industries where it is recognised that the majority of agreements should be exempted, for example certain types of vertical agreements

 Make your answer stand out

Regulation 1/2003 changed the existing system of individual notification and comfort letters. These procedures took a lot of the Commission's time, and so the Regulation devolved the matter down to national level. This was done by making Article 101(3) directly effective, and so it allowed companies themselves to resolve any problems in *national* courts of Member States. Cases decided under the old system are still relevant, and can still be used in answering assessment questions in this area. The system was brought into force on 1 May 2004, in time for the accession of ten new states – if it had not taken effect, then the Commission would probably have been completely overloaded with work from the new Member States.

The only drawback is that the Regulation has removed the comfort previously given by the Commission taking responsibility for this area. However, it has allowed national courts to deal with these matters.

If you are dealing with an issue in a problem question, please make sure that you do not advise the party concerned to get an individual exemption as this is now no longer relevant. If you are addressing an essay question which asks you to critically discuss the subject, then you can make your answer stand out by showing that you appreciate the change in this area. Knowing a little bit about the previous system may allow you to show an appreciation of the change that has taken place.

See Roitman (2006), Saunders (2006) and Venit (2003).

> **✎ EXAM TIP**
>
> Although Article 101 presents itself as a list of criteria to fulfil, it is still important to make sure you are able to discuss examples from the cases. Examiners will be looking for depth of knowledge, and the amount you understand of how Article 101 operates will come through in your answer.

■ Article 102 TFEU: abuse of a dominant position

> **KEY STATUTE**
>
> **Article 102(1) TFEU**
>
> Any abuse by one or more undertakings of a dominant position within the common market or in a substantial part of it shall be prohibited as incompatible with the common market in so far as it may affect trade between Member States.

Unlike Article 101, Article 102 tends to involve just one company abusing a strong position in the marketplace in which it is working. (It can involve several companies working together to produce a combined dominance.) Therefore, in order to deal with this area, you need to define several important elements. Article 102 just requires:

■ an undertaking (see the definition under Article 101);

■ a dominant position;

■ abuse of that dominant position;

■ effect on trade between Member States.

If all of these elements are present, then there is a breach of Article 102.

Market dominance

> **KEY CASE**
>
> **Case 27/76 *United Brands* v *Commission* [1978] ECR 207**
> *Concerning: definition of a dominant position*
>
> **Facts**
>
> United Brands were importers of bananas. They imposed various terms on the companies they supplied, for example insisting that bananas were not sold while still green, charging different prices to different suppliers in different countries, and in some circumstances, refusing to supply bananas. They were accused by the Commission of abusing a dominant position in their market.

> **Legal principle**
>
> A dominant position was defined as being a position of economic strength which allowed two things: (i) the dominant undertaking to *hinder effective competition*, and (ii) the undertaking to *act independently* of its competitors and consumers.

In order to establish this dominance, it is important to look at the relevant market. For example, in *United Brands*, the court had to decide whether the relevant market was for bananas or more generally for fruit. To establish what the market is, you need to look at the following:

Market	Explanation
Relevant product market (RPM)	Two important factors: the ability to substitute your product for other similar products, and the similarity of your products to other products
Geographical market	You need to consider how large a geographical area the company operates in. It must be 'the common market or a substantial part of it'

These issues then feed into a consideration of how dominant the undertaking is. For example:

- Case 27/76 *United Brands* v *Commission*: United Brands were dominant because the RPM was 'bananas', and not more generally 'fruit'. Bananas were different enough from other fruit for them not to be cross-substitutable. In considering this issue, you need to bear in mind something called 'demand-side substitutability'. Other fruit could not be substituted for bananas, and this led to a very narrow market definition.

- Case T-83/91 *Tetra-Pak* v *Commission* [1994] ECR II-755: the relevant geographical market was the whole of the EU.

- *B & I Line* v *Sealink Harbours & Stena Sealink* [1992] 5 CMLR 255: because the market concerned the control of harbours (rather limited because of the number of harbours in the EU) then a single harbour was a substantial part of the geographical market.

- Cases C-241/91 and C-242/91P *RTE and ITP* v *Commission*: the market here was defined as the market for TV listings information on BBC and RTE programmes, and therefore was narrow as in *United Brands*.

- Case T-229/94 *Deutsche Bahn AG* v *Commission*: in this case, the relevant market was for the carriage of marine containers by rail and therefore was very specific.

Dominance as a fact

These factors then feed into the issue of dominance as a fact. This can be as simple as merely having more of a share in the market than anyone else. It can be a case of having a larger share of the market than everyone else combined. Here are some examples:

Case	Situation of dominance
Case 85/76 *Hoffmann la Roche* v *Commission* [1979] ECR 1869	70–80% share in the market
Case 27/76 *United Brands* v *Commission* [1978] ECR 207	40–45% share in the market
Case T-219/99 *British Airways* v *Commission* [2004] All ER (EC) 1115	39.7% share in the market, where the nearest competitor, Virgin, had 5.5% share

✎ EXAM TIP

Dominance can be relative, as shown by the *British Airways* case in the table above. BA had less than half the share in its market than Hoffmann la Roche did in its case, but because BA's nearest rival had a much smaller share, it was still dominant. Think when you consider whether an undertaking is dominant, rather than just seeing if they have the majority (over 50 per cent) of the market.

! Don't be tempted to . . .

Don't think that the market share in itself is the only consideration when looking at market dominance. There are other considerations that the Court will also take into account when considering this issue. This includes the possibility of the undertaking having large financial resources (either its own, or access to other monies) or the possibility of having a technological advantage over competitors and therefore the ability to stay ahead in product development.

Abuse

Dominance on its own is *not* a breach of Article 102. However, the abuse of that dominant position is. There is a non-exclusive list of examples in Article 102.

KEY STATUTE

Article 102(2) TFEU

Such abuse may, in particular, consist in:

(a) directly or indirectly imposing unfair purchase or selling prices or other unfair trading conditions;

(b) limiting production, markets or technical development to the prejudice of consumers;

> (c) applying dissimilar conditions to equivalent transactions with other trading parties, thereby placing them at a competitive disadvantage;
>
> (d) making the conclusion of contracts subject to acceptance by the other parties of supplementary obligations which, by their nature or according to commercial usage, have no connection with the subject of such contracts.

The *United Brands* case is such a good case to apply here, because they were actually doing all four of the things listed above! There are other examples, though, and some of these are listed in the table overleaf.

The key thing to remember here is that all of these are examples of where someone has a dominant position, and is doing something which is abusive that exploits that dominant position. This is the key to breach of Article 102. Also bear in mind that the CJEU (formerly ECJ) has said that activities which allow an undertaking to achieve dominance that would be damaging to competition are also covered by Article 102 – see Case 6/72 *Europemballage and Continental Can* v *Commission* [1975] ECR 495.

Case	Abuse
Case 226/84 *British Leyland* v *Commission* [1986] ECR 3263	Unfair prices: charging more for approval certificates for left-hand drive cars
Case 238/87 *Volvo* v *Eric Veng* [1988] ECR 6211	Limiting the market: use of intellectual property rights to prevent competitors from producing spare parts for Volvo cars
Case T-219/99 *British Airways* v *Commission* [2004] All ER (EC) 1115	Discrimination: use of a dominant position in the market for travel agents to discriminate between levels of commission paid to agents
Case 85/76 *Hoffmann la Roche* v *Commission* [1979] ECR 1869	Tying in: a tying-in clause stopped suppliers from buying from Hoffmann's competitors, and allowed them to control the market
Case T-70/89 *Radio Telefis Eireann* v *Commission* [1991] ECR II-485	Refusal to supply: RTE and BBC refused to license TV listings information to competitors, therefore preventing competition for TV listings magazines

Make your answer stand out

The *RTE* case above seems to have led to an 'essential facilities doctrine', where if an undertaking refuses to license or supply (on reasonable terms) something which is considered an 'essential facility' for the emergence of a secondary market, then this can also be an abuse. This has a particular effect on those companies that produce things which cannot be reproduced by their competitors. This appears to put a higher level of control on companies that are in this position. Bear this in mind if dealing with a problem question that appears to involve a company that makes something that its competitors cannot make themselves.

See Stothers (2001).

Effect on trade between Member States

The effect of a breach on trade between Member States seems to have been very widely construed, as with Article 101, to prevent it obstructing the use of Article 102. Any effect on the market between Member States is enough.

✎ EXAM TIP

The issues of the market and whether a company is dominant or not are ones to be dealt with on an individual basis, so it is important for you to be able to *apply* the law rather than just present the criteria in your answer.

■ Putting it all together

Answer guidelines

See the essay question at the start of the chapter.

Approaching the question

The question itself appears to be very specific in its focus, but don't let this mislead you. A wider appreciation of Article 101 and how it operates will also need to be discussed in order to allow you to evaluate how Regulation 1/2003 has affected the way in which it works.

Important points to include

You will need to discuss:

- The requirements of Article 101, in particular the criteria for breach of this Article.
- The type of agreements considered to breach Article 101.
- The exceptions listed under Article 101(3), and don't forget that you will need to think of examples that may be relevant from the case law.
- Examples of how these have been applied under the previous system of comfort letters and individual notification.
- The consequences of removing control over Article 101 from the Commission – see Regulation 1/2003 – is it an advantage or a disadvantage that the system of comfort letters is no longer in operation? What were the good points of the previous system?

 Make your answer stand out

The temptation here will be merely to follow the flow diagram provided in this chapter and take a 'write everything you know about' approach to answering this question. However, this will not address the core of what it is asking you, and therefore you need to think about how the working knowledge you have of Article 101 allows you to produce an informed answer. Also – *very* importantly – your appreciation of how the law has developed here will also help. A sophisticated appreciation of how the law has changed, and why, will help you to show you have a critical understanding of this area. This is one of those areas that has been changed by the introduction of new rules, and therefore it gives you the advantage of not only examining the reasons behind the change just brought in, but also to examine the previous system and consider whether such a change was necessary to fix its shortcomings.

READ TO IMPRESS

Korah, V. (1980) 'Concept of a Dominant Position Within the Meaning of Article 86', 17 CML Rev 395

Roitman, D. (2006) 'Legal Uncertainty for Vertical Distribution Agreements: The Block Exemption Regulation 2790/1999 (BER) and Related Aspects of the New Regulation 1/2003', 27 ECLR 261

Saunders, O.O.R. (2006) 'Regulation 1/2003 – An Effective Mechanism for Managing Economic and Monetary Union in an Enlarged Community?', 27 Bus LR 148

▶

Stothers, C. (2001) 'Refusal to Supply as Abuse of a Dominant Position: The Essential Facilities Doctrine in the European Union', 22(7) ECLR 256

Venit, J.S. (2003) 'Brave New World: The Modernisation and Decentralisation of Enforcement under Articles 81 and 82 of the EC Treaty', 40 CMLR 545

Vogelaar, F. (2005) 'European Competition Law Revisited: The "Great Overhaul" of 2004 Analysed', 32 Legal IEI 105

www.pearsoned.co.uk/lawexpress

Go online to access more revision support including quizzes to test your knowledge, sample questions with answer guidelines, podcasts you can download, and more!

And finally, before the exam . . .

By using this book to direct your revision, you should now have a good grasp of the way in which the EU operates, the way it affects the law of Member States, and several key areas of substantive law. Remember that the information contained in this guide is not intended to substitute for your own notes and textbook reading, but to help to point you in the right direction when using these sources, which are going to have much more depth and detail than can be included here, as well as more case examples. Most importantly, you should check to make sure you have *understood* the different topic areas covered, as this will be crucial to success. It is not enough merely to learn or memorise information in this subject; you also need to be able to show you understand how it has developed, and how it applies to real situations.

Test yourself

- [ ] Look at the **revision checklists** at the start of each chapter. Are you happy that you can now tick them all? If not, go back to the particular chapter and work through the material again. If you are still struggling, seek help from your tutor.

- [ ] Attempt the **sample questions** in each chapter and check your answers against the guidelines provided.

- [ ] Go online to **www.pearsoned.co.uk/lawexpress** for more hands-on revision help and try out these resources:

  - [ ] Try the **test your knowledge** quizzes and see if you can score full marks for each chapter.

  - [ ] Attempt to answer the **sample questions** for each chapter within the time limit and check your answers against the guidelines provided.

  - [ ] Listen to the **podcast** and then attempt the question it discusses.

  - [ ] **'You be the marker'** and see if you can spot the strengths and weaknesses of the sample answers.

  ▶

☐ Use the **flashcards** to test your recall of the legal principles of the key cases and statutes you've revised and the definitions of important terms.

☐ If you are having problems with case names, remember that they are often abbreviated in a common way by all textbook writers and lecturers: e.g. *R* v *Secretary of State for Transport, ex parte Factortame* is commonly just referred to as '*Factortame*'.

☐ If you are allowed to take a statute book into the exam, make sure you are familiar with the Treaties, and their numbering. All Articles relating to a particular subject tend to be grouped together in the TFEU: e.g. all powers of the European Commission are contained in Articles 244–250 TFEU, and all Articles relating to the free movement of goods and customs union are in Articles 28–36.

■ Linking it all up

Check where there are overlaps between subject areas. (You may want to review the 'revision note' boxes throughout this book.) Make a careful note of these as knowing how one topic may lead into another can increase your marks significantly. Here are some examples:

✔ Overlap between one of the free movement areas and Article 258, because this question will be about both the law itself and the action that can be taken to enforce that law.

✔ Sources of law areas can overlap with Article 267 (interpretation by the CJEU), because this will concern the way in which an individual may be able to enforce law in national courts.

✔ Questions concerning the powers of the Institutions can overlap with specific procedures that may be used by those Institutions – e.g. Article 263 (judicial review) is a specific example of how any of the primary Institutions can exercise their powers to supervise the other Institutions' activities.

■ Knowing your cases

Make sure you know how to use relevant case law in your answers. Use the table below to focus your revision of the key cases in each topic. To review the details of these cases, refer back to the particular chapter.

Key case	How to use	Related topics
Chapter 1 – Sources and application of EU law		
Case 6/64 *Costa* v *ENEL*	To show that EU law is supreme over national law and so takes precedence	Direct effects
Macarthys v *Smith*	To show the effect that the UK's membership of the EU has on UK law	Direct effects
R v *Secretary of State for Transport, ex parte Factortame (No. 2)*	To show how conflicts in national law are dealt with by EU law	Interpretation of EU law; indirect effects
Case 26/62 *Van Gend en Loos* v *Nederlandse Administratie der Belastingen*	To demonstrate the criteria needed in order for a Treaty Article to be directly effective	Free movement of goods; the EU Single Market
Case 41/74 *Van Duyn* v *Home Office*	To demonstrate criteria used to show when EU law generally is directly effective	Free movement of persons; derogations from free movement principles
Case 14/83 *von Colson* v *Land Nordrhein-Westfalen*	To show the application of indirect effect	Direct effect
Litster v *Forth Dry Dock*	To show how indirect effect has been applied in the UK	Supremacy of EU law
Cases C-6 & 9/90 *Francovich* v *Italy*	To show the criteria needed to establish State liability for non-implementation of EU law	Damages for State liability
Chapter 2 – The Institutions of the EU and the decision-making process		
No relevant cases		
Chapter 3 – Articles 258–260 TFEU: Enforcement actions against Member States		
No relevant cases		

▶

Key case	How to use	Related topics
Chapter 4 – Articles 263 & 265 TFEU: Judicial review		
Case 25/62 *Plaumann* v *Commission*	For the definition of non-privileged applicants with individual concern under the rules for *locus standi* in judicial review	Customs duties; free movement of goods
Cases 106 & 107/63 *Alfred Toepfer and Getreide-Import Gesellschaft* v *Commission*	To show how the definition of 'fixed closed class' has been applied to importers	Customs duties; free movement of goods
Case T-18/10 *Inuit Tapiriit Kanatami* v *European Parliament*	To demonstrate the definition of 'regulatory Act' under Article 263(4)	Free movement of goods
Case T-262/10 *Microban International Ltd* v *European Commission*	To show a case where the definition of 'regulatory Act' was successfully applied	Free movement of goods
Case 246/81 *Lord Bethel* v *Commission*	To show how *locus standi* is applied with regard to non-privileged applicants under Article 265 (failure to act)	Competition law
Chapter 5 – Article 267 TFEU: Preliminary rulings in the CJEU		
Arsenal Football Club v *Reed*	To demonstrate the principle that Article 267 is split so that the CJEU interprets and the national court applies the law	
Case 246/80 *Broekmeulen* v *Huisarts Registratie Commissie*	To demonstrate the definition of 'court or tribunal'	
Commissioners of Customs & Excise v *Samex ApS*	To show where the CJEU has dismissed cases where Article 267 is just being used as a delaying tactic	

Key case	How to use	Related topics
Case 283/81 *CILFIT and Others* v *Ministro della Sanitá*	To show reasons for justifying a refusal to make a reference where a court would otherwise be obliged to do so	
Cases 28–30/62 *Da Costa en Schaake NV* v *Nederlandse Belastingadministratie*	To demonstrate the application of the *acte clair* principle	
R v *Henn & Darby*	To demonstrate the application of the *acte clair* principle	Free movement of goods under Article 34, derogations from FMOG under Article 36

Chapter 6 – Free movement of goods part 1: Taxes, duties and charges

Case 26/62 *Van Gend en Loos* v *Nederlandse Administratie der Belastingen*	To give an example of where a Member State has breached Article 30 through use of customs tariffs	Direct effects of Treaty Articles
Case 7/68 *Commission* v *Italy – Re: export tax on art treasures*	To show that Member States' justifications for imposing customs tariffs is irrelevant	
Cases 2 & 3/69 *Sociaal Fonds voor de Diamondarbeiders*	To show that a customs tariff breaches Article 30 even if there is no domestic market; to show that breaches of Article 30 cannot be justified	
Case 24/68 *Commission* v *Italy*	For the definition of charges equivalent to customs duties	
Case 132/82 *Commission* v *Belgium*	To show that charges on imports for a genuine service are allowed under Article 30	
Case 243/84 *John Walker* v *Ministeriet for Skatter*	To demonstrate the application of the definition of 'similar goods' under Article 110(1)	

▶

Key case	How to use	Related topics
Case 168/78 *Commission v France*	To demonstrate the application of the definition of 'competing goods' under Article 110(2)	
Case 170/78 *Commission v UK*	To demonstrate the application of the definition of 'competing goods' under Article 110(2)	

Chapter 7 – Free movement of goods part 2: Quantitative restrictions and MEQRs

Case 8/74 *Procureur du Roi* v *Dassonville*	The *Dassonville* formula defines an MEQR	
Case 120/78 *Rewe-Zentral AG* v *Bundesmonopolverwaltung für Branntwein* (*Cassis de Dijon*)	To apply the rule of reason and the rule of mutual recognition when deciding whether an indistinctly applicable MEQR is a breach of Article 34	
Cases C-267 and C-268/91 *Keck & Mithouard*	To show how an MEQR may not be a breach of Article 34 if it is a 'selling arrangement'	

Chapter 8 – Free movement of persons

R v *Secretary of State for the Home Department, ex parte Vitale and Do Amaral*	To demonstrate the limits of rights under EU citizenship	
Case C-299/95 *Kremzow* v *Austria*	To establish that EU citizenship is not a blanket concept in the same way as national citizenship is	
Case C-184/99 *Grzelczyk* v *Centre Public d'aide sociale d'Ottignies-Louvain-la-Neuve*	To demonstrate the operation of Article 18 in relation to EU citizenship	Discrimination on grounds of nationality
Case 66/85 *Lawrie-Blum* v *Land Baden-Württemburg*	To explain the definition of 'worker' under Article 45	

Key case	How to use	Related topics
Case C-292/89 *R* v *Immigration Appeal Tribunal, ex parte Antonissen*	To show the status of 'work seekers' under Article 45	
Case 222/86 *UNECTEF* v *Heylens*	To demonstrate the assessment of non-professional qualifications for freedom of establishment	Free movement of workers
Case 41/74 *Van Duyn* v *Home Office*	To show the use of derogations to excuse breach of Article 45 based on an individual's behaviour	
Case 30/77 *R* v *Bouchereau*	To show the relevance of previous criminal convictions when deciding whether derogation from Article 45 is applicable	
Case 67/74 *Bonsignore* v *Oberstadtdirektor of the City of Cologne*	To show that derogation from Article 45 must be based on a person's 'likelihood to re-offend'	

Chapter 9 – Competition law

Key case	How to use	Related topics
Case C-159/91 *Pucet* v *Assurances Générales de France*	To demonstrate the definition of 'undertaking' under Article 101	
Cases 11, 40–48, 50, 56, 113–114/73 *Suiker Unie* v *Commission*	To demonstrate the meaning of 'concerted practice' under Article 101	
Cases 56 & 58/64 *Consten* v *Commission*	To show the types of agreements that have been shown to be contrary to Article 101; to show that this includes vertical and horizontal agreements	
Case 27/76 *United Brands* v *Commission*	To define 'dominant position' under Article 102	

■ Sample question

Below is an essay question that incorporates overlapping areas of the law. See if you can answer this question drawing upon your knowledge of the whole subject area. Guidelines on answering this question are included at the end of this section.

ESSAY QUESTION

On 1 March 1999 the European Commission resigned to avoid the European Parliament exercising its power of censure against it. This power is a key aspect of the checks and balances system that has been developing at EU level with the changes made by Treaties over the past 30 years.

Discuss this system and evaluate how satisfactory it is at monitoring the activity within the EU.

Answer guidelines

Approaching the question

This question is designed to pull in several subjects and test your ability to draw links between the different areas of EU law in a discussion of the system. It is focused upon the supervisory powers of the Institutions, but in order to fully answer the question, you also need to make sure that other overlapping areas are also covered.

Important points to include

The following are issues you will need to consider in dealing with this question:

- The system the question mentions has developed with changes made by the Single European Act, the Maastricht Treaty, the Treaty of Amsterdam, the Treaty of Nice and the Treaty of Lisbon.

- Specific examples from the above Treaties focus on the powers of the Parliament, so discuss their powers of supervision and censure over the Commission, and possible reasons behind it, and their powers to monitor the Council of Ministers through questioning.

- The Council of Ministers also has its own powers, for example, their power of appointment of the Commission.

- The increased involvement of the Parliament in making law has allowed it to have a greater say in the law-making process, so you can discuss how the procedures have evolved into the Ordinary Legislative Procedure and the Special Legislative Procedure, as well as the Parliament's role in each of the different versions of these procedures.

- Articles 263 and 265 (judicial review) allow any of the Institutions to challenge improper procedural actions under the Treaty and also form part of the system of checks and balances. The grounds for challenge are relevant here, and therefore it will allow you to evaluate how effective this is as part of the system of checks and balances.

- Your evaluation of the EU system will dictate the answer you produce – but it is worth bearing in mind that although this is a question which covers several areas, you should remain focused upon the question. This is not about writing everything you know about this area – it requires a critical discussion.

 Make your answer stand out

This is an ever-changing area, particularly at the moment, due to the speed of EU reform. Therefore your answer won't necessarily be the same as that provided by students in previous years. You must make sure that you take account of the Lisbon reforms, and make sure that your information in revising for exam questions is up-to-date. By making your knowledge as current as possible, you will be able to show you have taken on board all the recent changes. An appreciation of the effect of politics upon the EU will help you produce a high quality answer.

Glossary of terms

The glossary is divided into two parts: key definitions and other useful terms. The key definitions can be found within the chapter in which they occur as well as in the glossary below. These definitions are the essential terms that you must know and understand in order to prepare for an exam. The additional list of terms provides further definitions of useful terms and phrases which will also help you answer examination and coursework questions effectively. These terms are highlighted in the text as they occur but the definition can only be found here.

■ Key definitions

Acte clair	A condition under which an issue of EU law is clear and does not need to be clarified by the CJEU.
Court of last instance	In a court structure, this is the very last or highest court that a particular case can reach.
Court or tribunal	Generally, a court or tribunal is one that has a judicial function, and independence from the parties concerned.
Customs duties	Customs duties are charges imposed at the point that goods cross a national boundary. Because of this they are an obstacle to goods moving from one EU country to another and are prohibited.
Democratic deficit	The accusation that the EU lacks democracy, due to a lack of democratic accountability to individual citizens. This has been partially addressed by the direct elections in the European Parliament.
Derogation	The exemption from, or the relaxation of, a particular law.
Dualist	A dualist legal system is one where international agreements also have to be passed by the national parliament.
Goods	Goods are interpreted as 'products which can be valued in money and which are capable, as such, of forming the subject

of commercial transactions' (Case 7/68 *Re Export Tax on Art Treasures: Commission* v *Italy* [1968] ECR 423 at 428).

Horizontal effect	A piece of EU legislation has horizontal effect where it is enforceable by an individual against another individual.
Indistinctly applicable measures	These are restrictions or other measures which apply equally to imported products and domestic products.
Legislative power	The power of the Institutions to make law.
Making a reference	Under Article 267, where a national court sends questions to the CJEU for interpretation.
Negative duty	A duty not to do something.
Qualified majority voting	Qualified majority voting is a form of voting where a certain percentage of the total vote must be in favour, usually around two-thirds.
Reasoned opinion	Under Article 258, the reasoned opinion is a written statement from the Commission which lays down the obligation concerned, and the reasons why the Member State has failed to meet this obligation. It should clearly spell out the Commission's objection, and therefore it should be possible for the Member State to know what it needs to do to rectify this situation.
Supervisory power	The power of the Institutions to supervise each other.
Undertakings	This is intended to cover only private individuals, and so it means natural persons (such as you and I) or legal persons (companies). However, in the context of Article 101, it has also been defined as groups of companies too.
Vertical effect	A piece of EU legislation has vertical effect where it is enforceable by an individual against the State.
Worker	Workers are EU nationals who are either in employment (full or part time) in that they are paid in return for their performance under an employer/employee relationship, or are seeking actual paid work.

◼ Other useful terms

Acquis communitaire	The existing body of EU law, all cases and legislation, both primary and secondary.
Adversarial	A procedure where the parties concerned present their own evidence and the Court decides the case based upon this.

EU Act	Any legislation made under EU law, whether Treaties or secondary legislation under Article 288.
Locus standi	A condition under which an individual or other entity has the permission or status to bring a case before the CJEU.
MEQR	Measures equivalent to quantitative restrictions.
Primary legislation	In the EU context, this is Treaty law agreed by the Member States.
Secondary legislation	Law made by the Institutions under the powers given to them in Article 288.
Unity principle	This is the principle where both Articles 263 and 265 are dealt with consistently by the CJEU.

Index

Emboldened entries refer to those appearing in the glossary.